ACCLAIM FOR DAVID SEDARIS'S

Squirrel Seeks Chipmunk

"Wickedly funny. . . . Sedaris has such a distinctive voice — which he brings, economically, to the page. . . . These are some of Sedaris's best stories — with twists that are improper or even nasty. The imbalance of good and evil feels contemporary, unlike the sanitized fairy tales we've grown used to in popular culture. This mix — of not-nice with playful and predictable — keeps the collection surprising. The animals have given Sedaris's humor some new teeth: tiny and sharp, and sometimes even ready to draw blood."

— Carolyn Kellogg, *Los Angeles Times*

"Sedaris has been called the funniest man on the planet. . . . This fictional collection of wonderfully twisted animal tales includes a sycophantic baboon, a cuckolded Irish setter, and a rabbit who becomes a tyrant when he tastes power."

— Pam Kelley, *Raleigh News & Observer*

"Sedaris's newest work is a departure from his usual autobiographical, self-deprecating essays, though his signature humor still dominates these stories. . . . The gorgeous illustrations of Ian Falconer . . . add to the fun that seeps through the pages of this collection."
— Courtney Crowder, *Chicago Tribune*

"The kind of magic that raises a shiver at once scary and satisfying. . . . Elegantly illustrated. . . . Sedaris is in fine form in these fables, creating slyly appropriate voices for his critters and keeping the stories streamlined, with just enough well-chosen detail to surprise and engage us — right up until he makes us gasp."
— Colette Bancroft, *St. Petersburg Times*

"Sedaris has become, to a certain portion of America, the most beloved living humorist."
— Monica Hesse, *Washington Post*

"David Sedaris, humorist and personal essayist extraordinaire, takes on selfishness, bigotry, righteousness, loneliness, and other all-too-human foibles in seventeen animal fables, à la La Fontaine and Aesop. They are as hilarious and slyly trenchant as his beloved stories about his sisters, SantaLand, and smoking. . . . You've got to love a writer whose empathy extends even to a sensitive potbellied pig. . . . What drives these stories, of course, is Sedaris's quirky sense of detail and inimitable voice."

— Heller McAlpin, National Public Radio

"In a departure from his signature confessionals, Sedaris joins the pack with this collection of animal-centric tales . . . and reminds us of every toxic relationship we've ever witnessed. . . . The humor here is black, the lessons disturbing."

— Judith Newman, *People*

"Wildly entertaining and reminiscent of the humor featured in his previous works. . . . He shows the insanity of everyday life through animal parodies in typical Sedaris fashion — blending sarcastic dialogue with mocking characters. He introduces star-crossed lovers who are prone to prejudices — those that are hilarious and unjust — and clearly a commentary on society. . . . *Squirrel Seeks Chipmunk* judges society, but it is also inviting and realistic. The satirical animals created in this short-story collection are sure to entertain Sedaris fans."

— Megan Roth, *Pittsburgh Post-Gazette*

"Hilarious yet poignant fables. . . . Through his furry protagonists Sedaris manages to broach topics ranging from racism to homophobia in a way that is at once engaging, irreverent, and — par for the David Sedaris course — uproariously funny. Finding the ever-elusive comfort zone where he tackles complex and controversial topics that provoke not only thought but a great deal of laughter, Sedaris proves that he has what it takes to chase some serious 'tale.' "

— Joseph Hassan, *Out Magazine*

"Perhaps you're thinking that Sedaris — witty, deft observer of the human condition — has shifted course. . . . But the bestselling humorist's book is about animals the way George Orwell's *Animal Farm* was about animals. . . . Charmingly subversive — and funny. . . . A dark twist on Aesop's fables."

— Jim Sullivan, *Boston Herald*

"Sedaris is a brilliant pathologist, dissecting foibles, anxieties, and pettiness with his hilariously understated prose. . . . Sedaris's bestiary is something different: It's a collection of animal tales, yes, and it is deeply moral in its concerns, but it doesn't

have the kind of preachy tone we expect from La Fontaine or Aesop. Instead of being a collection of clichés, Sedaris's animals have moral existences as complex and conflicted as humans'. . . . Exquisite insight into our elaborate self-justifications and self-deceptions. Just don't make the mistake of buying it for your animal-loving nine-year-old niece."
— Matt Frassica, *Louisville Courier-Journal*

"Literary joy. . . . No doubt, Aesop would have been proud." — Cary Darling, *Fort Worth Star-Telegram*

"Sedaris, long a droll chronicler of human foibles, turns his absurdist wit and opposable thumbs to fables of the feathered and four legged. . . . For the strong-stomached, these tales are toxic little treats, fun-size Snickers bars with a nougaty strychnine center."
— Leah Greenblatt, *Entertainment Weekly*

"Brainy . . . absurdist. . . . At times ribald or poignant and often funny, *Squirrel Seeks Chipmunk* finds Sedaris getting droll retribution against people who irritate him, and he's got a long list to work from."
— Suzanne Van Atten, *Atlanta Journal-Constitution*

"Some stories are humorous. Others are heart-breaking. Occasionally, they're both at the same time." — Bill Lynch, *Charleston Gazette*

"It's hard to pinpoint what about David Sedaris's writing is so brilliant, so funny, so adored. . . . It's a wild pairing of talent and a terribly clever idea."
— Holly Silva, *St. Louis Post-Dispatch*

"A bleakly funny story collection. . . . Think Aesop's fables, but with quite a bit more bite and blood from the bestiary."
— Richard Helm, *Ottawa Citizen*

Squirrel Seeks Chipmunk

Squirrel Seeks Chipmunk

A Modest Bestiary

David Sedaris

Illustrations by Ian Falconer

BACK BAY BOOKS

Little, Brown and Company

New York Boston London

Back Bay Books / Little, Brown and Company
Hachette Book Group
237 Park Avenue, New York, NY 10017
www.hachettebookgroup.com

Originally published in hardcover by Little, Brown and Company, September 2010
First Back Bay paperback edition, October 2011

Back Bay Books is an imprint of Little, Brown and Company. The Back Bay Books name and logo are trademarks of Hachette Book Group, Inc.

Acknowledgment is made to Public Radio International's *This American Life,* on which the following stories were originally broadcast in a slightly different form: "The Cat and the Baboon," "The Squirrel and the Chipmunk," "The Cow and the Turkey," "The Parrot and the Potbellied Pig," and "Hello Kitty." "The Cow and the Turkey" also appeared in *Holidays on Ice.*

Photo credits: surgical glove hand (p. 91) by Burke / Triolo Productions / Brand X Pictures (RF) / © Getty Images; hand with syringe (p. 91) © Fotosearch / George Doyle and Ciaran Griffin; hand throttling chicken (p. 108) © courtyardpix / Fotolia

The characters and events in this book are fictitious. Any similarity to real persons, living or dead, is coincidental and not intended by the author.

The publisher is not responsible for websites (or their content) that are not owned by the publisher.

Library of Congress Cataloging-in-Publication Data
Sedaris, David.
    Squirrel seeks chipmunk : a modest bestiary / by David Sedaris ; illustrations by Ian Falconer. — 1st ed.
    p.cm.
ISBN 978-0-316-03839-3 (hc) / 978-0-316-03840-9 (pb)
1. American wit and humor. 2. Bestiaries. I. Falconer, Ian. II. Title.
PS3569.E314S68 2010
813'.54 — dc22   2010026162

10 9 8 7 6 5 4 3 2 1

RRD-C

Printed in the United States of America

FOR MY SISTER GRETCHEN

Contents

CONTENTS

Squirrel Seeks Chipmunk

The Cat and the Baboon

The cat had a party to attend, and went to the baboon to get herself groomed.

"What kind of party?" the baboon asked, and she massaged the cat's neck in order to relax her, the way she did with all her customers. "Hope it's not that harvest dance down on the riverbank. My sister went last year and said she'd never seen such rowdiness. Said a fight broke out between two possums, and one gal, the wife of one or the other, got pushed onto a stump and knocked out four teeth. And they were pretty ones too, none of this yellowness you find on most things that eat trash."

The cat shuddered. "No," she said. "This is just a little get-together, a few friends. That type of thing."

"Will there be food?" the baboon asked.

"Something," the cat sighed. "I just don't know what."

" 'Course it's hard," the baboon said. "Everybody eating different things. You got one who likes leaves and another who can't stand the sight of them. Folks have gotten so picky nowadays, I just lay out some peanuts and figure they either eat them or they don't."

"Now, I wouldn't like a peanut," the cat said. "Not at all."

"Well, I guess you'd just have drinks, then. The trick is knowing when to stop."

"That's never been a problem for me," the cat boasted. "I drink until I'm full, and then I push myself away from the table. Always have."

"Well, you've got sense, then. Not like some of them around here." The baboon picked a flea from the cat's head and stuck it gingerly between her teeth. "Take this wedding I went to — last Saturday, I think it was. Couple of marsh rabbits got married — you probably heard about it."

The cat nodded.

"Now, I like a church service, but this was one of those write-your-own-vows sorts of things. Neither of them had ever picked up a pen in their life, but all of a sudden they're poets, right, like that's all it takes — being in love."

"My husband and I wrote our own vows," the cat said defensively.

"Sure you did," countered the baboon, "but you probably had something to say, not like these marsh rabbits, carrying on that their love was like a tender sapling or some damn thing. And all the while they had this squirrel off to the side, plucking at a harp, I think it was."

"I had a harp player at my wedding," the cat said, "and it was lovely."

"I bet it was, but you probably hired a professional, someone who could really play. This squirrel, I don't think she'd taken a lesson in her life. Just clawed at those strings, almost like she was mad at them."

"Well, I'm sure she tried her best," the cat said.

The baboon nodded and smiled, the way one must in the service industry. She'd planned to tell a story about a drunken marsh rabbit, the brother of the groom at last week's wedding, but there was no point in it now, not with this client anyway. Whatever she said, the cat disagreed with, and unless she found a patch of common ground she was sure to lose her tip. "You know," she said, cleaning a scab off the cat's neck, "I hate dogs. Simply cannot stand them."

"What makes you bring that up?" the cat asked.

"Just thinking," the baboon said. "Some kind of spaniel mix walked in yesterday, asking for a shampoo, and I sent him packing, said, 'I don't care how much money you have, I'm not making conversation with anyone who licks his own ass.' " And the moment she said it, she realized her mistake.

"Now, what's wrong with that?" the cat protested. "It's good to have a clean anus. Why, I lick mine at least five times a day."

"And I admire you for it," the baboon said, "but you're not a dog."

"Meaning?"

"On a cat it's . . . classy," the baboon said. "There's a grace to it, but a dog, you know the way they hunker over, legs going every which way."

"Well, yes," the cat said. "I suppose you have a point."

"Then they slobber and drool all over everything, and what they don't get wet, they chew to pieces."

"That they do." The cat chuckled, and the baboon relaxed and searched her memory for a slanderous dog story. The collie, the German shepherd, the spaniel mix she claimed to have turned away: they were all good friends of hers, and faithful clients, but what would it hurt to pretend otherwise and cross that fine line between licking ass and simply kissing it?

The Migrating Warblers

The yellow warbler would often claim that she was fine until she hit Brownsville. "Then — wham!" she'd tell her friends. "I don't know if it's the air or what, but whenever we pass it on our migration, I have to stop and puke my guts out."

"Indeed she does," her husband would say, laughing.

"An hour or two's rest is all I need, but isn't it strange? Not Olmito or Bayview or Indian Lake, but Brownsville. Brownsville every time."

The birds she was talking to would try to sound sympathetic or, at the very least, interested. "Hmmmm," they'd say, or, "Brownsville, I think I have a cousin there."

From the southern tip of Texas, the couple would fly over Mexico and then into Central America. "My family's been wintering in Guatemala for as long as I can remember," the warbler would explain. "Every year, like clockwork, here we come by the tens of thousands — but do you think any of those Spanish-speaking birds have bothered learning English? Not on your life!"

"It's really horrible," her husband would say.

"Well, funny too," his wife would insist. "Horrible *and* funny. Like one time I asked this little Guatemalan bird, I said, *'Don day est tass las gran days mose cass de cab eyza?'*"

Here her listeners would cock their heads, confused and more than a little impressed. "Wait a second, you *speak* that stuff?"

"Oh, I've picked some up," the warbler would say in that offhand way of hers. "I mean, really, what choice do I have? I guess I'm a pretty quick study. At least I've been told I am."

"She's terrific with languages," her husband would boast, and his wife would raise a wing in protest: "Well, not *always*. In this particular case, for instance, I thought I'd asked where all the big horseflies were. A reasonable question, only instead of *cob ayo,* which is "horse," I said *cab eyza.* So what I really asked was 'Where are all the big *head* flies?' "

Thinking that this was the end of the story, her listeners would quake with polite laughter. "Head flies, oh, that's rich!"

"But no, *wait,*" the warbler would say. "So the Guatemalan bird makes a motion for me to follow him through the thicket. I do, and there in this field are, like, three hundred heads rotting in the afternoon sun. Each one with about fifty flies on it. And I mean huge, the size of bumblebees, every one of them."

"Oh my God," the listeners would say. "Rotting heads with flies on them?"

"Oh, they weren't *bird* heads," the warbler would reassure them. "These belonged to humans, or used to anyway. Flesh bubbling off, hair all tangled with bits of goo in it. I don't know what they'd done with the bodies, burned them, maybe. Then they used the heads to make a wall."

"Actually, it was more like a counter," her husband would say.

It was a wall if ever there was one, but what could you do, ask everyone to stop up their ears while you and your ridiculous mate — someone who had never even *seen* a counter except in pictures — scream at each other for half an hour? No. It was best just to breeze over it.

"So we see this wall, this counter, be it, made of human heads, and I mean to say, 'This place stinks like the devil,' but what I actually say is . . ." And here, snorting with laughter, she would pass the baton to her husband.

"What she actually says to this small Guatemalan bird is 'The devil smells me in my place.' Can you believe it? My mate, Ladies and Gentlemen, or, as we like to call her south of the border, 'Satan's sexy stinkpot!' "

The listeners would crack up, and the warblers, husband and wife, would enjoy the sensation of having an audience right where they wanted them. This was the reward for spending three months a year in an inferior country. And when the light fell a certain way, when the laughter surged and melded into a harmonious song, it almost made up for all the hardships — the stomach flus, for instance, or the times when, rather than uniting you and your mate, the strangeness of another culture only made you feel more separate, more despicable and alone.

Back in their element, the two warblers were a well-oiled machine. "You want funny, try getting *work* done down there," the husband would say, opening the door to their hilarious tales of lazy natives, of how bumbling they were, how backward and superstitious. This begged the question "Why go in the first place? Why not winter in Florida like everyone else?" The warblers would then explain that despite the incompetence, despite the language barriers and the severed heads, Central America was, in its own way, beautiful.

"And cheap," they would add. "Cheap, cheap, cheap."

The Squirrel and the Chipmunk

The squirrel and the chipmunk had been dating for two weeks when they ran out of things to talk about. Acorns, parasites, the inevitable approach of autumn: these subjects had been covered within their first hour, and so breathlessly their faces had flushed. Twice they had held long conversations about dogs, each declaring an across-the-board hatred of them and speculating on what life might be like were someone to put a bowl of food in front of *them* two times a day. "They're spoiled rotten is what it comes down to," the chipmunk had said, and the squirrel had placed his paw over hers, saying, "That's it exactly. Finally, someone who really *gets* it."

Friends had warned them that their romance could not possibly work out, and such moments convinced them that the skeptics were not just wrong but jealous. "They'll never have what we do," the squirrel would say, and then the two of them would sit quietly, hoping for a flash flood or a rifle report — something, anything, that might generate a conversation.

They were out one night at a little bar run by a couple of owls when, following a long silence, the squirrel slapped his palm against the tabletop. "You know what I like?" he said. "I like jazz."

"I didn't know that," the chipmunk said. "My goodness, jazz!" She had no idea what jazz was but worried that asking would make her sound stupid. "What kind, exactly?" she asked, hoping his answer might narrow things down a bit.

"Well, all kinds, really," he told her. "Especially the earlier stuff."

"Me too," she said, and when he asked her why, she told him that the later stuff was just too late for her tastes. "Almost like it was overripe or something. You know what I mean?"

Then, for the third time since she had known him, the squirrel reached across the table and took her paw.

. . . .

On returning home that evening, the chipmunk woke her older sister, with whom she shared a room. "Listen," she whispered, "I need you to explain something. What's jazz?"

"Why are you asking me?" the sister said.

"So you don't know either?" the chipmunk asked.

"I didn't say I didn't know," the sister said. "I asked you why you're asking. Does this have anything to do with that squirrel?"

"Maybe," the chipmunk said.

"Well, I'm telling," the sister announced. "First thing tomorrow morning, because this has gone on long enough." She punched at her pillow of moss, then repositioned it beneath her head. "I warned you weeks ago that this wouldn't work out, and now you've got the whole house in an uproar. Waltzing home in the middle of the night, waking me up with your dirty little secrets. Jazz indeed. Just you wait until Mother hears about this."

The chipmunk lay awake that night, imagining the unpleasantness that was bound to take place the following morning. What if jazz was squirrel slang for something terrible, like anal intercourse? "Oh, I like it too," she'd said — and so eagerly! Then again, it could just be mildly terrible, something along the lines of Communism or fortune-telling, subjects that were talked about but hardly ever practiced. Just as she thought she had calmed herself down, a new possibility would enter her mind, each one more horrible than the last. Jazz was the maggot-infested flesh of a dead body, the crust on an infected eye, another word for ritual suicide. And she had claimed to like it!

Years later, when she could put it all in perspective, she'd realize that she had never really trusted the squirrel — how else to explain all those terrible possibilities? Had he been another chipmunk, even a tough one, she'd have assumed that jazz was something familiar, a kind of root, say, or maybe a hairstyle. Of course, her sister hadn't helped any. None of her family had. "It's not that I have anything against squirrels per se," her mother had said. "It's just that this one, well, I don't like him." When pressed for details, she'd mentioned his fingernails, which were a little too long for her taste. "A sure sign of vanity," she warned. "And now there's this jazz business."

That was what did it. Following the sleepless night, the chipmunk's mother had forced her to break it off.

"Well," the squirrel had sighed, "I guess that's that."

"I guess it is," the chipmunk said.

He headed downriver a few days later, and she never saw him or heard from him again.

"It's not a great loss," her sister said. "No girl should be subjected to language like that, especially from the likes of him."

"Amen," her mother added.

Eventually the chipmunk met someone else, and after she had safely married, her mother speculated that perhaps jazz was a branch of medicine — something like chiropractic therapy — that wasn't quite legitimate. Her sister said no, it was more likely a jig, and then she pushed herself back from the table and kicked her chubby legs into the air. "Oh, you," her mother said, "that's a cancan," and then she joined in and gave a few kicks of her own.

This stuck in the chipmunk's mind, as she never knew her mother could identify a dance step or anything associated with fun. It was the way her own children would eventually think of her: dull, strict, chained to the past. She had boys, all of them healthy, and only one prone to trouble. He had a habit of being in the wrong place at the wrong time, but his heart was good, and the chipmunk knew he would eventually straighten himself out. Her husband thought so too, and died knowing that he had been correct.

A month or two after he'd passed on, she asked this son what jazz was, and when he told her it was a kind of music, she knew instinctively that he was telling the truth. "Is it bad music?" she asked.

"Well, if it's *played* badly," he said. "Otherwise it's really quite pleasant."

"Did squirrels invent it?"

"God, no," he said. "Whoever gave you that idea?"

The chipmunk stroked her brown-and-white muzzle. "Nobody," she said. "I was just guessing."

When her muzzle grew more white than brown, the chipmunk forgot that she and the squirrel had had nothing to talk about. She forgot the definition of "jazz" as well and came to think of it as every beautiful thing she had ever failed to appreciate: the taste of warm rain; the smell of a baby; the din of a swollen river, rushing past her tree and onward to infinity.

The Toad, the Turtle, and the Duck

The complaint line started at the edge of the swamp and stretched westward, ending, where the turtle finally arrived, at the base of a charred pine stump. He fell into place behind a glassy-eyed toad and had just commenced a jaw-aching yawn when a duck showed up

and took the position behind him, muttering, "What a bunch of idiots."

The turtle, his mouth still open, nodded in agreement.

"This is my second time in this line, can you believe it?" groused the duck. "First they told me I wouldn't need any ID, then, after I waited almost three hours, this ball-busting river rat goes, 'I'm sorry, sir, but if you don't have some form of identification, there's nothing I can do.'

"I was, like, 'Why the hell didn't you tell me that earlier?' And she was all, 'If you can't be civil, I'm afraid I'm going to have to ask you to leave.' "

The turtle groaned in sympathy, as something similar had once happened to him. "It's the oldest trick in the book," he said. "*They* screw up, but somehow *you're* the problem."

"I said to her, 'You want civil, try working for a company that doesn't give everyone the goddamn runaround!' " the duck continued. " 'You can't very well complain about our complaining when you're the one who's given us something to complain about.' "

"Well put," said the turtle, who was, he'd later admit, genuinely impressed. "You don't expect such clarity from a duck, or any bird, really, but this one totally nailed it," he'd tell his wife when he got home that evening.

It was here that the toad entered the conversation. "You want pissed off? I got to the front of the line, I showed my ID, and I was then told that I needed *two* forms of it. Can you beat that? I said, 'I didn't see that ugly-assed bobcat give you two forms,' and the one behind the counter, a black snake, she was, said that this was a special rule just for reptiles.

"I said, 'No problem, I'm an amphibian.' And to this she goes — I kid you not — 'Same difference.'

"I said, 'It's not the same fucking difference. First off, I only mate in the water. Number two, the skin I was born with — I still got it. So don't feed me any of that "same difference" bullshit. You should know that better than anyone.'

"Then she gives me the same line of crap the river rat gave this duck, all, 'I'm sorry, sir, but if you're going to use that kind of language . . .' "

The turtle rolled his eyes. "Typical."

"I should have punched her," the toad said. "Right in the face — pow."

"I'm with you, brother!" said the duck.

"Or no," continued the toad, "I should have

gouged out her eyes, blinded her so she had to spend the rest of her life in darkness."

The turtle had a blind cousin, a cousin he hated, and this made him laugh all the harder.

"Then I should have yanked out her tongue," the toad said. "See how she liked that!"

"Not so easy giving us shit when she can't talk," said the duck.

"After all that, I should have set her on fire," added the toad. "No, I should have poured acid on her and then set her on fire, the stupid bitch."

The turtle started saying something, but the toad, excited by a new possibility, interrupted him: "Or wait, no, after cutting off her tongue, I should have smeared an apple with shit, opened up her big fat mouth, and forced it down her throat. *Then* I should have poured acid on her. *Then* I should have set her on fire."

The three of them laughed.

"Better yet, you should have used a cantaloupe," said the turtle. "Cover that with shit and stuff it down her throat. Ha!"

"Or no," said the duck. "Instead of a cantaloupe, you should have used a watermelon. Then you —"

And here the merry atmosphere soured. "A watermelon for the black snake," said the toad. "Now you're just being a racist."

"No," the duck said, "I only meant —"

"I know what you 'meant,' " the toad said, "and I think it stinks."

"Hear! Hear!" agreed the turtle.

"Yeah, well, to hell with the both of you," said the duck, and he waddled off, muttering under his breath.

"God, I hate guys like him," the toad said. "A watermelon. He wouldn't have said that if she'd been a king snake, and he damn sure wouldn't have said it if she were a python."

The pair looked at the retreating duck and shook their heads in disgust. A moment of silence, and then the toad continued, "I should have smeared a honeydew with shit — or no, a honeydew *and* a cantaloupe. I should have smeared both melons with shit and forced them down her throat. *Then* I should have poured acid on her, and *then* I should have set her on fire."

"Well," said the turtle, "there's always the next time."

The Motherless Bear

In the three hours before her death, the bear's mother unearthed some acorns buried months earlier by a squirrel. They were damp and worm-eaten, as unappetizing as turds, and, sighing at her rotten luck, she kicked them back into their hole. At around ten she stopped to pull a burr from her left haunch, and then, her daughter would report, "Then she just . . . died."

The first few times she said these words, the bear could not believe them. Her mother gone — how could it be! After a day, though, the shock wore off, and she tried to recapture it with an artfully placed pause and an array of amateur theatrical gestures.

The faraway look was effective, and eventually she came to master it. "And then," she would say, her eyes fixed on the distant horizon, "then she just . . . died."

Seven times she cried, but as the weeks passed this became more difficult, and so she took to covering her face with her paws and doing a jerky thing with her shoulders. "There, there," friends would say, and she would imagine them returning to their families. "I saw that poor motherless bear today, and if she doesn't just break your heart, well, I don't know what will."

Her neighbors brought food, more than enough to get her through the winter, so she stayed awake that year and got very fat. In the spring the others awoke from their hibernations and found her finishing the first of the chokecherries. "Eating helps ease the pain," she explained, the bright juice dripping from her chin. And when they turned away she followed behind them. "Did I mention to you that my mother died? We'd just spent a beautiful morning together, and the next thing I knew —"

"That's no excuse for eating all our chokecherries," they said, furious.

A few bears listened without interruption, but she could see in their eyes that their pity had turned to something else, boredom at best, and at worst a kind of embarrassment, not for themselves but for her.

The friend who had previously been the most sympathetic, who herself had cried upon first hearing the story, now offered a solution. "Throw yourself into a project," she said. "That's what I did after my grandfather's heart attack, and it worked wonders."

"A project?" the bear said.

"You know," said her friend, "dig yourself a new den or something."

"But I like my den the way it is."

"Then help dig one for somebody else. My ex-husband's aunt lost one of her paws in a trap and spent last winter in a ditch. Help her, why don't you?"

"I hurt my paw once," the bear said. "Broke a nail clean off, and when it finally grew back it looked like a Brazil nut." She was trying to work the subject back to herself, hoping her friend might forget her suggestion, but it didn't work.

"I'll tell the old gal you'll be by later this afternoon," she said. "It'll make her happy and help you to work off some of that weight you've gained."

The friend ambled off, and the bear glared at her disappearing backside. "Help you work off some of that weight you gained," she mimicked.

Then she overturned a log and ate some ants, low-calorie ones with stripes on their butts. After that, she lay in the sun and was sound asleep when her friend returned and shook her awake, saying, "What's wrong with you?"

"Huh?"

"It's almost dark, and my ex-husband's aunt has been waiting all day."

"Right," said the bear, and she headed up the hill, deciding after a few dozen yards that this was not going to happen. Forget following advice she had never asked for in the first place. Rather than digging a den for a stranger, someone old who was just going to die anyway, she'd leave home and settle on the other side of the mountain. There, she could meet some new bears, strangers who would listen to her story and allow her once again to feel tragic.

The following morning she set out, taking care

to avoid the old amputee, who still sat waiting beside her wretched ditch. Beyond a burned-out grove of birch trees there was a stream, and, following it, she came upon a cub who sat waist-deep in the rushing water, swatting at fish with his untrained paws.

"I used to do the same thing when I was your age," called the bear. And the cub looked up and let out a cry of surprise.

"I must have sat in the water all morning, until my mother came over and showed me how to catch fish properly." She waited a beat and then continued. "Of course, that could never happen now, and you know why?"

The cub said nothing.

"It couldn't happen now because my mother is dead," the bear announced. "Happened suddenly, when I least expected it. One moment she was there, and the next she just . . . wasn't."

The cub began to whimper.

"You wake up an orphan, your mom's body slowly rotting beside you, and what can you do but soldier on, all alone, with no one to love or protect you."

As the cub began to wail, his mother charged out of the thicket. "What are you, sick?" she shouted. "Get your kicks scaring innocent children, is that it? Go on, now, get the hell out of here."

The bear ran to the opposite shore and into the forest, tripping on logs as she turned to look behind her. What with her weight, she was soon out of breath, so she slowed to a trot after the first hundred yards, her pace gradually degenerating as the morning turned to afternoon and then early evening. Just before dusk she smelled chimney smoke and ambled to the outskirts of a village. Peering through a gap in a thick hedge, she saw a crowd of humans standing with their backs to her. They seemed to be regarding something that stood in a clearing, and when one of them shifted position, she saw that it was a bear, a male, though it took a moment to realize it, as he was wearing a skirt and a tall, cone-shaped hat topped with a satin scarf. The male bear's mouth was muzzled with leather straps and connected to a leash, which was alternately held and yanked by a man in a dirty cape. A boy who was also dressed in a cape carried a drum on a rope around his neck, and as he began to play, the male stood on his hind legs and swayed back and forth to the music.

"Faster," called a soldier at the front of the crowd, and the boy quickened his beat. The male bear struggled to keep up, and when he tripped over the hem of his skirt, the man pulled out a stick and beat him across the face until his nose bled. This made the people laugh, and a few of them threw coins, which the drummer collected before moving on to his next song.

When night fell and the audience went home to their suppers, the man removed the muzzle from the male's snout. Then he put a collar around his neck and attached it by a chain to an iron stake driven deep into the ground. He and the boy retired to a tent, and when she was sure they had fallen asleep, the bear crept out from behind the hedge and approached the chained dancer.

"I don't normally talk to strangers," she said, "but I saw you here and figured, well, I guess there's a first time for everything."

The male was lying in an awkward position. His skirt was gathered around his waist, and she saw that great patches of his legs were without hair and that the skin in these areas was covered with open sores. "I used to talk a lot to my mother," she told him. "She and I were all each other had, and then one morning, out of nowhere, she just . . . died. Gone. Before I could say goodbye or anything." Maybe it was the moonlight, maybe the excitement of meeting an entertainer, but for whatever reason, she actually managed a tear — her first in almost six months. It was running slowly down her cheek when the chained male raised his head and spoke. "Can you understand me?" he asked.

The bear nodded, though in fact it was quite difficult.

"That's good," he said. "Most animals can't make out a word I'm saying, and you know why?"

She shook her head.

"It's because I have no teeth," he said. "Not a one of them. The man in the tent took a rock and hammered them out of my head."

"But the muzzle —," the bear said.

"That's just to make me look dangerous."

"Oh," the bear said. "I get it."

"No," he told her, "I don't think you do. See, I

have maggots living in my knees. I'm alive, but flies are raising families in my flesh. Okay?"

The bear shivered at the thought of it.

"It's been years since I've eaten solid food. My digestive system is shot, my right foot is broken in three places, and you're coming to me all teary-eyed because your stepmother died?"

"She wasn't a *step*," the bear said.

"Oh, she was too. I can see it in your eyes."

"Well, she was *just like* a real mother," the bear said.

"Yeah, and piss is just like honey if you're hungry enough."

"Maybe males in this part of the country say every ugly thing that enters their heads," the bear said, "but where I'm from —" That was as far as she got before the man and the boy came up from behind and hit her over the head with a padded club. When she came to, it was morning, and the male lay on the ground before her, his throat slit into a meaty smile.

"He wasn't no good to us anyhow," the man said to his assistant. "The knees go, and that's that."

Now the bear travels from village to village. Her jaws are sunken, her gums swollen with the abscesses left by broken teeth, and between the disfigurement and the muzzle, it's nearly impossible to catch what she's saying. Always, though, while tripping and stumbling to the music, she looks out into her audience and tells the story about her mother. Most people laugh and yell for her to lift her skirts, but every so often she'll spot someone weeping and swear they can understand her every word.

The Mouse and the Snake

Plenty of animals had pets, but few were more devoted than the mouse, who owned a baby corn snake — "A rescue snake," she'd be quick to inform you. This made it sound like he'd been snatched from the jaws of a raccoon, but what she'd really rescued him from was a life without her love. And what sort of a life would that have been?

"I saw him hatching from his little egg and knew right then that I had to save him," she was fond of saying. "I mean, look at that face! How could I have said no!" The snake would flick his split ribbon of tongue, and his mistress would dandle the scales beneath his chin. "He's saying, 'Hello, new friend. Nice to meet you!' "

But the friends weren't so sure. When the serpent coiled, they jumped and fretted, reactions that left the mouse feeling almost unbelievably special — exotic, really, which was different from eccentric. To qualify for the latter, all you needed was a turban and an affinity for ridiculously large beads or the color purple. To be exotic, on the other hand, one had to think not just outside the box but outside the world of boxes.

"You're not afraid of my snake," the mouse would insist. "You're afraid of the *idea* of him. Why, this little fellow wouldn't strike if his life depended on it. Haven't I explained that?" She'd then describe how he slept at the foot of her bed and woke her each morning with a kiss. "He says, 'Get up, Mommy. It's time to start the day!' "

The snake was the smartest, the handsomest, the most thoughtful creature that had ever lived. The way he lay in the sun or stared dumbly into space for hours on end — it was uncanny. "He thinks he's one of us," the mouse told her friends, who responded with increasingly forced smiles. In time she stopped using the word "pet," as it seemed demeaning. The term "to own" was banished as well, as it made it sound as though she were keeping him against his will, like a firefly trapped in a jar. "He's a reptile companion," she took to saying, and thus, in time, he became her only companion.

This suited the mouse just fine. "I never had anything in common with them anyway," she said. "Not even the ones my own age." The snake blinked as if to say, *All we need is each other,* and the mouse reached out to hug his slender neck. It was almost spooky how like-minded they were: On the weather, on the all-important hoard or binge question, the two were most definitely on the same page. Both liked weekends, both hated owls; their opinions differed only when it came to food. "Won't you at least *try* a bit of grain?" the mouse had asked when the snake was very young. He wouldn't, though, preferring instead a live baby toad. How he could eat these things was beyond her. She'd taken a bite once, just to see what it was like, and the ghost of it, viscous and fishy, had lingered in her mouth for days.

You couldn't expect a youngster, especially such a vulnerable one, to hunt his own food, and so the mouse did it for him.

Aside from baby toads, she'd fetched him a robin's egg and a very young mole, which, like everything else, he ate whole. "My goodness," she said. "Slow down. Taste!"

In those first few months, their lunch was followed by a speech-therapy session. "Can you say, 'Hello, mouse friend'? Can you say, 'I love you'?"

Eventually she saw the chauvinism of her attempt. Why should he learn to speak like a rodent? Why not the other way around? Hence she made it her business to try and master snake. After weeks of getting nowhere she split her tongue with a razor. This didn't make it any easier to communicate, but it did give them something else in common.

The two were in front of the fireplace one afternoon, softly hissing at each other, when someone knocked on the door. It was a toad, and after a great sigh at the inconvenience, the mouse stepped onto the front stoop to greet her. Even without the mimeographed flyers under her arm, anyone could have guessed why she was here: it was that "long-suffering mother" look so common to amphibians, who had children by the thousands and then fell apart when a handful were sacrificed to a higher cause.

"I'm sorry to barge in on you this way," the toad said, "but a few of my babies has taken off and I'm just about at my wit's end." She blew her nose into her open palm, then wiped the snotty hand against her thigh. "They's girls as well as boys. Nine in all, and wasn't a one of them old enough to fend for themselves."

It was this last part that tested the mouse's patience — *fend for themselves* — as if a toad needed any particular training. They hatched, they opened their eyes, and then they hopped around, each one as graceless and unappealing as a stone.

"Well," the mouse said, "if you were that concerned for the safety of your children, you probably should have kept an eye on them."

"But I *did*," wept the toad. "They was just outside, playing in the yard, like youngsters do."

Playing indeed, thought the mouse, and she recalled the patch of sandy soil, bare but for a single, withered dandelion. The area bordered a thicket of tall ferns, and that was where she had hidden herself and lured the listless, gullible children with the promise of cluster flies. If they hadn't been starving, and possibly brain damaged due to their upbringing, they wouldn't have so blindly followed her. So really, wasn't this the toad's fault? Where was *her* pity when flies came to the door, asking about *their* missing babies? Was an insect's mother love any less worthy than an amphibian's? And wasn't the snake a baby as well, as cute and innocent and deserving of protection as any other living creature?

It pained the mouse to realize that, while he'd always be adorable, her companion was not the little one he had been. In the months since she'd rescued him, he'd grown almost five inches, and there seemed to be no stopping him. Underage toads would not suffice for much longer, and so the mouse accepted a leaflet and studied it for a moment. "I'll tell you what," she said. "How's about I keep my eyes open, and you check back with me in, oh, say, about two weeks or so. How does that sound?"

A few days later there came another knock, this time from a mole. "I'm wondering," she asked, "if you've by any chance seen my daughter?"

"Well, I don't know," the mouse said. "What did she look like?"

The mole shrugged. "Don't know exactly. I guess most likely she looked like me but smaller."

"It's a shame when things you love go missing,"

the mouse said. "Take these grubs, for instance. I had a whole colony living in my backyard, darlings, every one. And just so smart you couldn't keep up with them. One minute they were there, and the next thing I knew they'd taken off — no note or anything."

Her visitor looked at the ground for a moment, and the mouse thought, *Exactly.* If awards were given to the world's biggest hypocrites, you'd be hard-pressed to choose between the moles and the toads.

"To answer your question, I *did* meet a little mole," the mouse said. "A girl it was, said she'd run away from home and asked if she could come live with me for a while. I told her, 'Well, maybe you should think it over and not be so rash.' I said, 'Why don't you see how you feel in a month, and then come back?' "

"A month!" wailed the mole.

"That's what I told her, so why don't you do the same? If your daughter is here, I'll keep her for you, and if not, at least you tried."

Off went the mole, buoyed with hope, and the mouse stepped back into her house. "Idiot," she whispered. The snake lifted its flat head off the carpet, and she explained that from now on, his meals would deliver themselves. "That's all the more time we can spend together," she said. "Would you like that, baby? I know you would."

Out slid the snake's forked tongue, and she thought again that she had never seen such a beautiful creature. Smart too. Beautiful and smart, and above all loyal.

A month later the mole was back. She stood at the door, knocking politely, and just as she began pounding, the toad hopped by. "If you're looking for that mouse, I think you can probably forget it," she called.

The mole whirled around and squinted.

"I came by two weeks ago and did just what you're doing. Knocked on that door till I just about busted it, but didn't nobody answer. Then I talked to some squirrels yonder, and they said there hadn't been smoke out the chimney since the beginning of the month. Strange, they said, because that mouse always had a fire going, even in summer. Their guess and mine too is that she took off, maybe

found a mate or something. You know how mice are — anything for a little affection."

The mole, distressed, spilled out the story of her missing child. The toad did the same. But had they not wept and commiserated, had they instead put their ears to the door, they might have heard the snake, his belly full of unconditional love, banging to be let out.

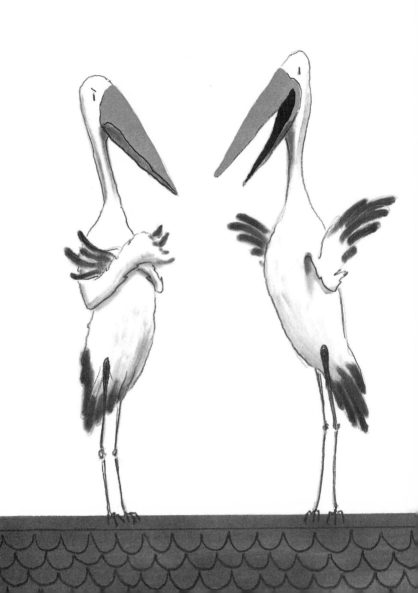

The Parenting Storks

The precocious stork was only two weeks old when he asked where babies come from.

"Goodness," said his mother. "I mean, golly, that's quite some question." She considered herself to be as modern as anyone, but didn't you have to draw the line *somewhere?* "Let me get back to you on that," she said, and she shoved a herring down his throat with a bit more force than usual.

Later that day the mother stork repeated the conversation to her sister, who also had a recently born chick. She meant it as a *Don't kids say the darnedest things* type of story and was unprepared for the reaction she got.

"Your only son came to you for answers, and you didn't give them to him?"

"Well, of course I didn't," the stork said. "Why, he's just a baby himself. How can he be expected to understand something so complicated?"

"So children should be put off or, even worse, *lied to?*"

"Until they're old enough, sure."

"So we lie and we lie and then one day they're just supposed to believe us?"

"That's how it was with *our* family, and I never felt particularly traumatized," the stork said. "Besides, they're not lies so much as stories. There's a difference."

"Oh, is there?" spat her sister, surprised at how angry this was making her. "Give me an example."

The stork squinted over the surrounding rooftops until something came to her. "All right. I remember seeing my first full moon and being told by Granddad that it was a distant natural satellite formed billions of years ago. And I believed it for the longest time until I learned the truth."

"The truth?" her sister said.

"God made it," announced the stork.

Her sister felt suddenly ill. "Who?"

"God," the stork repeated. "He made the world and the heavens, all of it out of dust and willpower, and in less than a week! I overheard a cardinal talking about him on top of the cathedral in the square, and it was really quite instructive."

"So is *that* who brings the babies? God?"

"Lord no," the stork said. "Babies are brought by mice."

It took a moment before her sister could speak. "Oh, sweetie," she said, "our babies are huge, so how on earth —"

"These are special mice," the stork explained. "Capable of lifting things much heavier than themselves. They hide until you lay your eggs, see, and then, when your back is turned, they slip the chicks inside."

"But we build our nests on chimney tops," the sister said. "How could a little mouse — a mouse carrying a live, vivacious newborn — climb that high? And how would he hold the chick while he did it?"

"Ever hear of magic pockets?" the stork asked.

"Magic mice pockets, sure," her sister said, and

she wondered how anyone so gullible could manage to feed herself, much less build a nest and raise a child. "And where exactly did you get this information?"

"Oh," said the stork, "just this guy I've been having sex with."

Now it was the sister's turn to stare over the rooftops. "I know," she said. "Why not tell your son *that's* where babies come from — sex. It's crazy, I know, but maybe it will tide him over until he's old enough to grasp that whole magic-mouse concept."

"You think so?"

"I do," her sister said.

The stork flew off, and her sister, shaken, watched her go. They'd both had the same parents and had both left the nest at roughly the same time. They lived in the same town and drank the same water, so how was it that she herself had turned out to be so smart, while her poor sister was so confused?

With the conversation still fresh in her mind, she returned to her own child, a female born ten days earlier. The chick opened her beak for food, and the stork sighed. "I know you're hungry, but Mother's had an exhausting afternoon and needs to recharge

her batteries before she puts on her slave hat." She picked a few feathers out of the nest and flicked them over the edge. "Do you want to know *why* Mommy's exhausted?"

The child opened her beak even wider, and the stork let out a moan. "It really wouldn't hurt you to take an interest in others," she said. "I tell you I'm depressed, I tell you I feel cornered and lonely, and your response is 'Fine. Now feed me,' which is actually very insensitive of you. All mothers feel unconditional love for their children, but there's a timer on it, all right. It doesn't last forever, especially when you're selfish."

The child closed her beak.

"Mommy's depressed because your cousin wanted to know where babies come from. Now, this is all perfectly natural for someone your age — nothing at all to be ashamed of. Sex is a beautiful and important part of life, I explained that to you last week, when we discussed your father's infidelity. Remember we talked about Daddy's cheating? I told you that there were good lovers and bad ones and that your father is pathologically inattentive to the needs of his partners. I said that you were not conceived of mutual orgasm and that it probably affected your ability to empathize, remember?"

A crow flew by, and, keeping her head perfectly still, the child followed it with her eyes.

"It's caring too deeply that has gotten me depressed, not about you so much as your aunt, who told me with great authority that babies are brought by mice."

The child's eyes widened.

"That was my reaction as well," said the stork. She looked at her daughter and, for the first time in days, felt a splinter of hope. Then, deciding she was hungry, she flew off in search of food.

The chick watched her go and wished once again that she had a brother or sister, someone, anyone, besides her mother, who never for one moment stopped talking about herself. She'd thought since birth that she was fated to be an only child, but maybe the mice could change that. The question was: How did they work? Did they visit every nest in turn? Was it possible that they took requests and would come when charmed or summoned? The chick leaned over the edge of the nest, hoping to see one of these mice and call out to it. Then she leaned out a little farther.

ul Setter

Back before I met her, my wife lived on a farm. It was a small operation, organic vegetables, pick-your-own strawberries, and a dozen or so chickens, each and every one of them, to hear her tell it, "an absolute raging asshole." The first time she said this

I laughed, as I'd always thought that word was reserved for males. The same goes for "dick," which she uses for females all the time — this raccoon, for example, that sometimes gets into our garbage cans. "Can you believe the nerve of that dick?" she'll say to me, her nose pressed flat against the dining room window. Then she'll bark, "Hey, asshole, go trash somebody else's fucking yard."

I attribute my wife's language to the fact that she's one-quarter spaniel. She says she's only an eighth, but, come on, the ears say it all. That and her mouth.

Still, though, I can't help but love her — forgave her even after she cheated. "They are *too* your children," she'd said, referring to her last litter, a party of four that looked no more like me than that dick of a raccoon. I knew they were fathered by the English bull terrier across the street, but what are you going to do? Everyone's entitled to one mistake, aren't they?

I'd like to tell you that I hated this terrier right from the start, that I'd never, for one moment, trusted him. But what would that say about my wife and me, that our tastes are *that* dissimilar? If you want to know the truth about it, I actually hadn't given the guy much thought. His ugliness I'd noticed, sure — those creepy little eyes. His stupidity was evident as well, but I can't say I'd fashioned a formal "opinion." At least not until this puppy business.

The litter was born, and not one week later the bull terrier bit a kid in the face, practically tore it right off, as a matter of fact. It was the little blond girl who lived in the house next door to him. I was in the backseat of the car, just pulling into the driveway, when the ambulance arrived, and, man, was that ever a scene. The parents were beside themselves.

"Oh well," my wife yawned when I told her about it later that afternoon. "It's not like they can't have more children."

I said, "Come again?"

She said, "That's the way they feel about *us*, so why should we be any different?"

"So we need to stoop to *their* level?" I said. As for the bull terrier, my wife admitted that he was a hothead. She said he had a lousy sense of humor, but she never quite denounced him the way I needed her to. After he was trundled away and put down, she spent the day sulking. "A headache," she said to the kids. "Mommy has a sick headache." She claimed to have one the following day as well. On and on for a week, and all the while she had her eye on the house across the street, the place where her boyfriend had lived.

It wasn't long afterward that the little girl came home from the hospital, her head cocooned in bandages. There were holes for her to look through, and others for her nose and mouth, all of them gunked up with their corresponding fluids: tears, snot, drool. Even if you hated children, you had to feel sorry for her. At least I thought you had to. My wife, though, I could see that she blamed this girl, thinking that were it not for her, the bull terrier would still be alive.

I figured she'd get over him eventually, and in the meantime I'd just settle back and be patient. It helped when our owner put an ad in the paper and got rid of those godforsaken puppies. Oh sure, I cried, but it was more for my wife than for myself. I don't care what you hear about stepparenting, it's just not the same when they're somebody else's kids.

Don't get me wrong — I wish them the best. I just don't feel the need to see them again.

Now that it was just the two of us, I hoped that things would return to normal. It was then that our owner took my wife in for a hysterectomy. She was out cold for the operation, saw nothing, felt nothing, went to sleep fertile and woke up a shell, her uterus and whatever else was in there, gone.

I told her that as far as I was concerned, it didn't matter in the least. To this she growled, "Oh, I'm sure it doesn't. I'm sure you're just *fine* with it."

I said, "What are you talking about?"

"You're thinking that this will keep me from cheating on you again. Or that if I do at least nothing will come of it."

It was like she was blaming me for the hysterectomy. I said, "Baby, don't do this."

She didn't talk to me for three days after that. What was going through her mind is anyone's guess. Me, though, I kept thinking about this Weimaraner I met once at the dog run. He had one of those owners who'd get on all fours and try to communicate with him, not just barking but lying on his back, acting submissive and so forth. There are quite a few people like that at the dog run — nuts is what they are — but this guy really took the cake. One morning last fall he went to the hospital and had his tonsils taken out. They weren't raw or swollen or anything, he just wanted them. "In a jar," he supposedly told the doctor. "And don't trim off the fat."

At the end of the day, he returned home, cut the tonsils into pieces with a steak knife, and hand-fed them to this Weimaraner, like, "Here, boy, I love you so much, I want you to have a part of me."

"And?" I said.

"It was a lot like chicken," the Weimaraner told me. So that's what I wondered during the time my wife and I weren't talking. *What did her hysterectomy taste like?* It was crazy, I know, but I couldn't get it out of my mind. Did my thoughts bespeak an urge toward cannibalism? Or did the flesh in question — the fact that it was her uterus — reduce this to a normal sexual fantasy? I would've liked to have discussed it, but the way things stood, I thought it best to keep my mouth shut.

It was right about then, my wife wanting her boyfriend back and me entertaining these insane, dark thoughts, that the bandaged girl reappeared. It seemed there were some complications, an infection or something, and she had to go back to the hospital. We saw her through the living room window, just briefly, getting into the car with her parents. "Little Miss Priss," my wife muttered — the first words out of her mouth in what felt like forever. Then she limped into the den and lay down in front of the TV. This is her way of being alone, as I hate the television. The programs are beside the point. It's the machine itself I can't bear. It stinks to high heaven, so I always stop at the doorway and park myself just this side of the carpet.

"That's right, Mr. Snob," my wife said. She always calls me that when we disagree about something, whether it's a chew toy or the smell of an electrical appliance. "I guess I'm just not as well-bred as you," she'll say. And it's true. She's not. It's also true that she's the one forever bringing it up. It's her own insecurity talking, the tragic self-hatred of a mixed-breed country girl, so I try to let it slide.

My wife mentions my bloodline when she's ticked off, of course, and then again whenever I get sent out on a stud call, which is not the same as cheating, I don't care what you hear. Infidelity involves a choice, while this is arranged by forces beyond my control. "These females don't want me any more than I want them," I tell my wife. "It's not an affair, it's work. It's my job, for God's sake."

She says that if it's a paycheck I'm after, I could just as easily lug around a blind person. "Or better yet, sniff out contraband, you and that selective nose that hates the TV but loves the smell of a book."

"Not *all* books," I tell her. And it's true. I can't stand thrillers.

It was in the midst of our difficulties, my wife's stitches still tender, that I was sent to service a female a few hours west of our home. Normally it's just "hello/good-bye," but the land is beautiful in that part of the world. It's wooded, with lots of hills, so rather than waiting for me to finish, my owner decided to drop me off and spend the rest of the day nosing around in his car. The act itself — it's hard to think of it as sex — lasted no more than a minute. Then this female and I got to talking. She's pure Irish setter, just like me, so we had that in common. Both of us had hookworms when we were young, and both of us, very coincidentally, love the taste and texture of candles. "As long as they're not scented," she said.

"The worst are those cheap *vanilla* candles," I offered.

She agreed, adding that the "cheap" part was redundant. "*All* vanilla-scented candles are cheap."

I told her about a cinnamon-scented candle I'd once chewed on as a puppy, and as she howled her sympathetic disgust, I thought of my wife and of how we would have sounded to her ears. "Arrogant," she'd have called us. "Noses so high in the air you can't smell your own farts." This for the crime of preferring one thing over another.

"You know what else I hate?" I said to the female. "I hate air fresheners, coconut being the worst."

"Well, I don't know," she said. "I think a pretty good case could be built against wild cherry."

"Oh my God, wild cherry!" I said, and I hunched my shoulders, pretending to barf.

From air fresheners, we wandered on to padded toilet seats, novelty mailboxes, and Labradoodles.

She'd just started in on light jazz when I suggested we try the breeding thing one more time. "In case the first go didn't work."

"Don't have to ask me twice," she said.

I didn't have to ask at all for round three, and the one after that just seemed to happen on its own. "An aftershock," the female called it. Some might define this as cheating, but I just call it being thorough. Then too I was completely up front about my marital status, practically from the start.

"Your wife?" the female said. "So how did *that* happen?"

I told her we were married by my owner's girlfriend. "Now former girlfriend," I said. "I don't know how binding it is, but I wouldn't want to be with anyone else." And it's true, I wouldn't. Among other things, I like the fact that my wife needs me. Without my guidance, she's sure to finish what her boyfriend started. The child across the street will be mangled even worse, and for what? "This is *not you*," I keep telling her. For now, though, it's as if she's under a spell. I explained this to the female as best as I could, and after I'd finished she cocked her head.

"So your wife was brainwashed by an English bull terrier?"

"Something like that."

"God," she said, "I *hate* English bull terriers."

That was when we had the aftershock.

It was almost dusk when the owner arrived, and he and I headed off for home. The air conditioner was on, but after some whining I got him to lower the window. I had my head out and we'd been on the road for no more than twenty minutes when we came upon a burning building. It was a house, three stories tall, with a low brick wall around it. The owner pulled over, and before he could stop me I jumped over the seat and joined him on the grass. Had my wife been with me, he'd have forced us back into the car, but I'm pretty reliable, even without a leash. Besides, I make him look good, much more interesting than he actually is.

A small crowd had begun to gather, encircling a barefoot woman with sweatpants on. As we moved closer, I saw that she was holding a dachshund, the type with long hair. Everyone watched as she pushed back his ears, repeatedly kissing his forehead while he twisted and begged to be let down. It was only when an old man arrived and gathered the woman in an embrace that the dog broke free. He and I got to talking, and I learned he was the single thing this woman had reached for when she smelled the smoke and realized that her house was on fire. "Which is nice and everything, don't get me wrong," the dachshund said, "but she's got a teenage son in there." He gestured toward a second-floor window with black smoke pouring out of it. "He and his mother were constantly at each other's throats, but he was always nice to me, poor kid."

The dachshund let out a sigh, and as the woman reached down to snatch him back up, I caught a glimpse of the poor guy's future. *I could have saved anything, and I chose you.*

Who wants to live with that kind of pressure?

As I wished him good luck, the firemen arrived. A group of three headed toward the house and were almost there when a part of the roof collapsed. Sparks shot into the darkening sky, and as they sputtered down to earth, I caught the scent of burning flesh and realized how hungry I was. With any luck the owner would stop on our way home and buy us each a hamburger wrapped in paper. Then, smelling of smoke and ketchup, I'd return to my hangdog wife and continue the long business of loving her.

The Crow and the Lamb

The crow was out one morning, looking for something to eat, when she spotted a newborn lamb suckling in the field below. *Sheep,* she thought. *What I wouldn't give for a life like that. The mother spits out a baby and then she just lies there doing nothing while it feeds itself. No nest to build, no spending every rotten moment searching for food, and even then it's never enough.*

On top of that, birds had to be homeschooled, not like sheep or cows, who learned junk from one another. "It takes a village," they liked to say, not that there was much to learn in the first place.

You lower your head, and food goes in. Raise your tail, and it comes out. The eating part, they had down, but the rest, forget it. Crap smeared from one end of their bodies to the other. Where was the fucking village when it came to cleaning themselves? That's what the crow wanted to ask. Oh, they moaned about the insects — flies lighting on their faces all day — but news flash: flies go where the shit is, so if you don't want them clustering on your forehead, clean it! God, these grazing animals were stupid, which was not altogether a bad thing.

After circling a few times, the crow landed in the pasture and pretended to pick at something in the grass. The old ewe looked her over for a moment, then returned her attention to the newborn, who was receiving the first and probably the only bath of its life. "Cute kid," the crow called out. "Is it a boy or a girl?"

The ewe sighed in the way of all parents who expect their baby's sex to be obvious. "*He's* a boy. My second." Normally she was more sociable, but something about birds put her off — their uselessness, she supposed.

"Well, he's an absolute lamb, if you don't mind

my saying so," the crow said, and she hopped a bit closer. "Tell me, was it a natural childbirth?"

The ewe had wanted to remain aloof, but what with the subject matter — that is to say, herself — she found it impossible to hold out for more than a few seconds. "Oh yes," she said. "A hundred percent natural, but then again, that's just my way. It makes it more 'real,' if you know what I mean."

The crow nodded. "And the placenta?"

"Oh," the ewe said, "I ate it. Tasted like the devil, but I think it's important for, you know, the bonding process."

"Definitely," the crow agreed, and she lowered her head to scowl into the grass. Nothing irritated her more than these high-and-mighty vegetarians who ate meat *sometimes* and then decided that it didn't really count. "So I suppose you choked down the umbilical cord as well?"

"Don't remind me," the ewe said, and she made a little gagging gesture. "Some of them are burying it now, holding a little ceremony, but then I heard that dogs dig it up, which sort of takes the godliness out of it, don't you think? I mean, don't get me wrong, I'm not a fanatic or anything. You won't catch me posing in any nativity scene, but I do consider myself to be a very spiritual being."

"That, I think, is much better than being quote/unquote 'religious,' " the crow said, and she took another step closer. "Rather than joining the blind followers, the sheep, if you'll forgive the expression, you've figured out what's right for you and gotten rid of the rest. Take shaving, for instance — some faiths say you can't do it. Now, that's fine for a horse or a chicken or whatnot, but where would it leave you?"

"I shudder to think." The ewe chuckled. "Especially in the summer heat!"

"Exactly," the crow said. "Why buy the whole package when it's just going to drag you down? I heard of another religion that says you can't touch a pig."

"Well, I'm in!" the ewe said, and she laughed again, revealing her thick, even teeth.

"I would be too, to tell you the truth," the crow confided. "But what if you were a pig yourself and your child needed feeding? What are you going to do? Send it to a cow? Let it starve to death?"

"I see your point," the ewe said.

"So we pick and we choose," the crow continued. "A little of this and a little of that. I, for example, have recently thrown some Oriental meditation into the mix. Every morning I shut my eyes for ten minutes or so and just sort of block it all out. The noise, the hubbub — everything, gone."

The ewe turned her head toward the far end of the field, squinting at the brook and the row of poplars that shifted lazily behind it. "I'm afraid we don't have much hubbub around here," she said. "It's a pretty quiet place compared to most."

"You've just gotten used to it is all," the crow told her. "The other sheep, the crickets and so forth, and if your baby is anything like mine, I bet he can really raise the roof when he wants a second helping."

"Oh yes."

"It might not seem like much, but taken as a whole, this farm racket can really jangle the nerves. And that's what meditation is all about. It's a way of saying, 'Back off, world. It's time for me to be good to me.' "

"I like the sound of that," the ewe said, and she looked at her baby, who was sitting upright with his legs folded beneath him, his eyes glued to her teats. "Tell me, though, is it hard, this . . . what did you call it?"

"Meditation," the crow said. "And to answer your question, it couldn't be easier. The first step is to close your eyes, good and hard, mind you, as peeking lets in bad energy that can seriously mess with your digestion."

The ewe did as she was told.

"Now, there's no set rule, but what the Orientals like to do is repeat what they call a mantra," the crow explained. "The same line over and over, until it really sinks into your spirit. It sounds boring, I know, but it's actually very effective."

"What kind of a line?" the ewe asked. "Like poetry or something?"

"Well, I suppose it could be," the crow said. "My own mantra is more of an affirmation, I guess you could call it. It's sort of personal, but you're more than welcome to use it if you like, at least until you come up with something of your own."

"It's not dirty, is it? I have the child to think about."

"Of course it's not dirty," the crow said. "I can't believe you would even ask such a question."

"I didn't mean to insult you," the ewe said. "It's just that, well, you hear stories . . ."

"And that means that all crows are filthy, does it? We've all got sex on the brain?"

"What I meant is that I'd love to borrow your mantra," the ewe said. "That is, if I still can."

The crow looked from the lamb to its mother, marveling that something so cute could grow to be so shapeless and ugly. It was just the opposite with birds, she thought. Nothing was more repellent than a chick, but then again, who needs looks when you're too young and stupid to use them? Keeping one's eyes shut would be a valuable skill for someone like the ewe, especially when it came time to mate. She pictured a ram heaving its battered, spindly legs upon her back, and then she shook her head to wash the image away. "I guess I'll let you use my mantra, but just until you come up with your own," she said, and she leaned forward to whisper it into the ewe's ear. "Now I want you to put your head down and repeat that line twenty times. No, better make it thirty, after everything you've been through."

The ewe did as she was instructed, and as she mumbled into the damp grass, the crow moved beside her and plucked out the eyes of the newborn lamb. One she ate right away, for it was delicious, and the other she set into her beak and carried back to her ungrateful children.

As for the ewe, she was still deep in meditation, her eyes clamped shut, repeating the code of thieves and charlatans and those who are good to themselves the world over. "I have to do what I have to do," she said. "I have to do what I have to do."

The Sick Rat and the Healthy Rat

The white rat had been sick for as long as he could remember. If it wasn't a headache, it was an upset stomach, a sore throat, an eye infection. Pus seeped from his gums. His ears rang, and what little he ate went right through him. Now came the news that he had pancreatic cancer, which was actually something of a relief. "Finally I can die," he moaned to his new roommate. She was a female, also white, and had arrived only that morning.

The tank they shared was made of glass, its walls soiled here and there with bloody paw prints and flecks of vomit. "Well," she sighed, wincing at the state of her new home, "I'm sorry to say it, but if you have a terminal illness it's nobody's fault but your own."

"I beg your pardon?" said the white rat.

The female approached the water bottle, stuck her paws into the spigot, and began to wash them. "It's nice to believe that these sicknesses just 'befall' us," she said. "We blame them on our environment and insist that they could happen to anyone, but in truth we bring them on ourselves with hatefulness and negativity."

The white rat coughed up some phlegm with bits of lung in it. "So this is *my* fault?"

"Oh, I think that's been proven," the female said. "You might not have realized how negative you were being — maybe you were passive-aggressive. Maybe no one cared enough to point it out, but I have to call things like I see them. Just as everyone does to me, only in the opposite direction. 'How come you're always so sunny?' they ask, and 'Doesn't your mouth hurt from all that smiling?' Some interpret it as overexuberance, but to me it's a kind of vaccine — as long as I'm happy and I love everybody, I can't get sick."

"Never?" asked the white rat.

"Oh, I had a flu once, but it was completely my own fault. Someone I mistook for a friend took to criticizing me behind my back — saying things regarding my weight and so forth. I got wind of it, and for all of three minutes I wished her ill. I'm not talking *death,* just a little discomfort — cramping, mainly. I was just starting to visualize it when I sneezed, which was my body's way of saying, 'Whoa,' you know, 'that's not cool.' Then my nose stopped up and I came down with a fever."

"And what about your supposed friend, the one who said cruel things behind your back? If you got a flu, what happened to her?" asked the white rat.

"Well, nothing yet," the female said. "But sometimes the body bides its time." Her pink eyes narrowed just slightly. "I can bet that when something *does* happen, though, it'll be a lot worse than a flu. Diabetes, maybe."

"You sound pretty hopeful," the white rat observed.

The female scowled, then smiled so hard the corners of her mouth touched her eyes. "Not at all. I wish her the best."

The white rat slumped against the wall and put

a hand to his forehead. "I can't think of anybody I dislike. Then too, I've been alone since my last roommate died."

"That's another cause of cancer," the female told him. "You need to get out, socialize. Storytelling is pivotal to our well-being, as are nonethnic jokes and riddles." Food pellets dropped from a chute beside the water bottle, and she took a bite of one. "I heard somewhere that limericks can cure both heart disease *and* certain types of cancer. Can you beat that? Limericks!"

The white rat knitted his brow.

"They're poems," the female explained. "You know, like, 'There once was a mouse *da da da* / who *da da da da da da da*.' "

"Oh, right," said the rat, and, silently recalling one about a prostitute and a dead cat, he chuckled. "And what about haiku? Are they good for curing *shorter* diseases?"

"I know when I'm being mocked," the female said, "but that's okay. You're sick and are going to die. I, meanwhile, am perfectly healthy with good teeth and a positive attitude toward life, so joke away if it makes you feel any better."

She'd just cracked open that smile of hers when

the mesh ceiling parted and a human hand appeared. At first it seemed to be made of wax, that's how rigid and opaque it was, but as it neared and pinned her to the floor, the female smelled rubber and understood that it was encased in a glove. Then came a second hand, this one bearing a hypodermic needle, and as the tip sank into her stomach, releasing its mad punch of viruses, the white rat settled against the wood chips and thought.

Most limericks, it seemed to him, involved a place. "There was a young mole from Des Moines," say, or "In Yorktown there once lived a ferret." He didn't know where he was, though. It was a lab, obviously, but the location was anyone's guess. With this in mind, he came up with the following:

A she-rat I had as a roomie
said illness just strikes if you're gloomy.
Since she was injected
with AIDS, I've detected
an outlook a lot less perfumy.

Funny, he thought, but it actually *did* make him feel better.

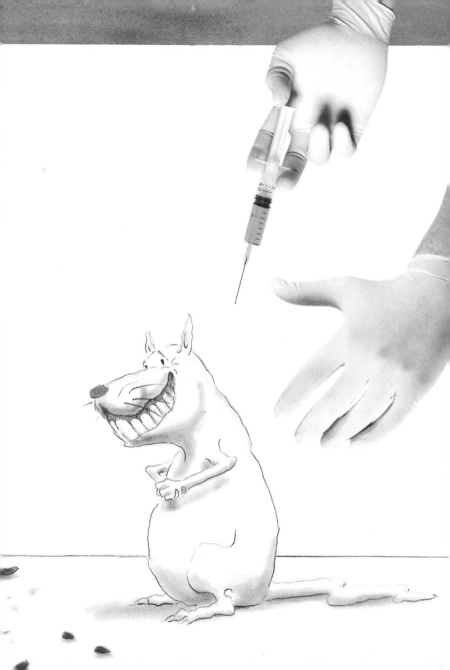

The Cow and the Turkey

The cow was notoriously cheap, so it surprised everyone when she voted yes for the secret Santa scheme. It was the horse's suggestion, and she backed it immediately, saying, "I choose the turkey."

The pig, who considered himself an authority on all things gifty, cleared his throat. "That's not actually the way it works," he said. "It's secret, see,

so we each draw a name and keep it to ourselves until Christmas morning."

"Why do you always have to be like that?" the cow asked, and the duck sighed, "Here we go."

"First you ask me to give someone a Christmas present," the cow continued, "and then you tell me it has to be done *your* way. Like, 'Oh, I have four legs so I'm better than everyone else.' "

"Don't *you* have four legs?" the pig asked.

The cow loosed something between a moan and a sigh. "All right, just because you have a curly tail," she said.

The pig tried looking behind him, but all he could see were his sides. "Is it curly *curly?*" he asked the rooster. "Or curly *kinky?*"

"The point is that I'm tired of being pushed around," the cow said. "I think a lot of us are."

This was her all over, so rather than spending the next week listening to her complain, it was decided that the cow would give to the turkey and that everyone else would keep their names a secret.

There were, of course, no shops in the barnyard, which was a shame, as all of the animals had money, coins mainly, dropped by the farmer and his plump, moody children as they went about their chores. The cow once had close to three dollars and gave it to a calf the family was taking into town. "I want you to buy me a knapsack," she'd told him. "Just like the one the farmer's daughter has, only bigger and blue instead of green. Can you remember that?"

The calf had tucked the money into his cheek before being led out of the barn. "And wouldn't you know it," the cow later complained, "isn't it just my luck that he never came back?"

She'd spent the first few days of his absence in a constant, almost giddy state of anticipation. Watching the barn door, listening for the sound of the truck, waiting for that knapsack — something that would belong only to her.

When it no longer made sense to hope, she turned to self-pity, then rage. The calf had taken advantage of her, had spent her precious money on a bus ticket and boarded thinking, *So long, sucker.*

It was a consolation, then, to overhear the farmer talking to his wife and learn that "taking an animal into town" was a euphemism for hitting him in the head with an electric hammer. *So long, sucker.*

Milking put the cow in close proximity to humans, much closer than any of the other animals, and she learned a lot by keeping her ears open: who was dating whom, how much it cost to fill a gas tank, any number of useful little tidbits — the menu for Christmas dinner, for instance. The family had spent Thanksgiving visiting the farmer's mother in her retirement home and had eaten what tasted like potato chips soaked in chicken fat. Now they were going to make up for it "big-time," the farmer's wife said, "and with all the trimmings."

The turkey didn't know that he would be killed on Christmas Eve; no one knew except the cow. That's why she'd specifically chosen his name for the secret Santa program — it got her off the hook and made tolerable his constant, fidgety enthusiasm.

"You'll never in a million years guess what I got you," she said to him a day after the names were drawn.

"Is it a bath mat?" the turkey asked. He'd seen one hanging on the farmer's clothesline and was promptly, senselessly, taken by it. "It's a towel *for the floor!*" he kept telling everyone. "I mean, really, isn't that just the greatest idea you've ever heard in your life?"

"Oh, this is a lot better than a bath mat," the cow said, beaming as the turkey sputtered, "No way!" and "What could possibly be better than a bath mat?"

"You'll see come Christmas morning," she told him.

Most of the animals were giving food as their secret Santa gift. No one came out and actually said it, but the cow had noticed them setting a little aside, not just scraps but the best parts — the horse her oats, the pig his thick crusts of bread. Even the rooster, who was the biggest glutton of all, had managed to sacrifice and had stockpiled a fistful of grain behind an empty gas can in the far corner of the barn. He and the others were surely hungry, yet none of them complained about it. And this bothered the cow more than anything. *Which of you is sacrificing for me?* she wondered, her mouth watering at the thought of a treat. She looked at the pig, who sat smiling in his pen, and then at the turkey, who'd hung a sprig of mistletoe from the end of his wattle and was waltzing from one animal to the next, saying, "Any takers?" Even to other guys.

Oh, how his cheerfulness grated on her. Waiting for Christmas Eve was murder, but wait the cow did, and when the time was right — just shortly after breakfast — she sidled up beside him. "You do know they'll be cutting your head off, don't you?" she whispered.

The turkey offered his strange half smile, the one that said both "You're kidding" and "Please tell me you're kidding."

"If it's not the farmer, it'll be one of his children," the cow confided. "The middle one, probably, the boy with the earring. There were some jokes about doing it with a chain saw, but if I know them they'll stick to the ax. It's more traditional, and we all know how they love a tradition."

The turkey laughed, deciding it was a joke, but then he saw the pleasure in the cow's face and knew that she was telling the truth.

"How long have you known?" he asked.

"A few weeks," the cow told him. "I meant to tell you earlier, but with all the excitement, I guess I forgot."

"Kill me *and* eat me?"

The cow nodded.

The turkey pulled the mistletoe from the end of his wattle. "Well, golly," he said. "Don't I feel stupid."

. . . .

Not wanting to spoil anyone's Christmas, the turkey announced that he would be spending the holiday with relatives. "The wild side of the family," he said. "Just flew in last night from Kentucky." Noon arrived, and when the farmer and his middle son appeared in the barnyard, the turkey went to them without a fuss, saying, "So long everyone" and "See you in a few days."

They all waved good-bye except for the cow, who lowered her head toward her empty trough. She was just thinking that a little extra food might be nice, when something horrible occurred to her. The rooster was standing in the doorway, and she almost trampled him on her way outside, shouting, "Wait! Come back. Whose name did you draw?"

"Say what?" the turkey said.

"I said, whose name did you get? Who's supposed to receive your secret Santa present?"

The turkey answered a thin, "You'll see," his voice a little song that hung in the air long after he'd disappeared.

The Vigilant Rabbit

A white-tailed doe was discovered one morning disemboweled on the banks of the stream, and the residents of the forest went crazy with fear — "freaked out" was how the sparrow put it. A few days later, a skunk was found, no more than a gnawed-upon skull attached to a short leash of spine. Personality-wise, he'd been no great shakes. Neither was he particularly good-looking, but still! Then a squirrel disappeared, and it was decided that something had to be done. A meeting was convened in the clearing near the big oak, and the hawk, who often flew great distances in search of food, proposed that they build a gate. "I've seen one where the humans live, and it seems to work fairly well."

"Work how?" asked a muskrat.

The hawk explained that once the gate was erected, anyone entering the forest would have to stop and identify himself. "It keeps out the riffraff," he said, adding that when bad things happened, that was usually who was responsible — riffraff.

For the second time that day, the muskrat raised his hand. "And what if this riffraff can't be stopped?"

"Then you sound an alarm," the hawk suggested. "It could be anything, really, just so long as it's loud."

The building of the gate was left to the beaver, who had a slight problem with the hinges but eventually got them right. Just to the side of them he hung a gong fashioned from an old NO TRESPASSING sign. "I figured I could hit it with my tail," he said, and he gave it a whack for good measure.

When the noise had stopped echoing off the surrounding hills, the rabbit stepped forward. "Who elected *you* to man the gate?" he asked, adding that anyone could hit a sheet of rusted metal, even someone without an oversize tail. At that he picked up a heavy stick and went at it, creating a racket as loud as the beaver's. "I've also got the better hearing," he boasted. "I'm slimmer, I'm faster, and I'm more safety conscious, *vigilant,* you might say."

All eyes turned to the beaver, who said simply, "Whatever," and waddled back to his lodge.

On the rabbit's first morning as chief of security, he stopped an approaching snake, who looked up at him and laughed until he cried.

"Something funny?" asked the rabbit.

The snake used his tail to wipe a tear from his face. "You idiots," he said. "What good is a gate without a wall?"

"What good is a *huh?*"

"It doesn't make any sense," continued the snake. "If an animal doesn't want to enter *here,* what's to stop him from moving down a few dozen yards and crawling in beside the fallen pine?"

"What's to stop him?" asked the rabbit, and he picked up his heavy stick and bashed the snake's head in. Then he kicked some dirt over the body and wrote NO LAUGHING on the NO TRESPASSING sign.

A short while later a magpie stopped by and pecked at the bits of brain left scattered on the ground in front of the gate. "Not to nitpick," he said between mouthfuls, "but what's to prevent someone from entering by air? You and your friends initiate a no-fly zone?"

"What's to keep you from flying in?" asked the rabbit, and once again he brought down his heavy stick. Then he dug up the snake and hung both it and the dead magpie from the top of his gate. There they could act as visual warnings, proof that he was a force to be reckoned with. When that was done, he added to his sign, which now read, NO TRESPASS-ING. NO LAUGHING. AND NO STUPID QUESTIONS EITHER. THIS MEANS YOU.

It was a hot, windless day, and within an hour blowflies arrived and settled on the faces of the two dead animals. Their buzzing attracted a frog, who jumped over from the nearby stream, flicked out his tongue, and dined upon them until he was full. Only then did he read the sign and turn to address the rabbit. "Seeing as you don't want jokes or questions, I guess I'll phrase this as a comment," he said. "In order to enter through your gate, I'll have to stop and go through your tiresome rigmarole. That kind of BS doesn't interest me much, so instead I'm going to return to my stream and *swim* into your third-rate, beetle-infested forest."

He turned to leave, and the rabbit, who was nothing if not quick, reached for his heavy stick. Then he hung the frog upon his gate and added NO CURSING to his NO TRESPASSING sign.

It wasn't long before an otter came along and went for the crushed frog. Then a badger stopped by, attracted by the smell of the dead otter. As the bodies were heaped upon the gate, it began to tilt. The rabbit propped it up with a fallen branch and then turned his attention to the sign. NO DIRTY LOOKS, he wrote. NO QUESTIONING MY INTEGRITY. NO INSULTING REMARKS ABOUT MY EARS OR MY TEETH. He was just wondering how to spell "insolence" when a shadow fell, and he looked up to see a magnificent white unicorn. His silky mane curled about his neck in waves the color of buttercups. Equally brilliant was his horn, which looked to be made of gold. At his approach, the rabbit put down his pencil. "State your name and your business."

"I'm a unicorn," said the unicorn, "and I come to bring joy to all the forest creatures."

"Not with that horn you don't," said the rabbit.

"I beg your pardon?"

"I said, lose the weapon."

"The horn is what makes me who I am!"

"Which is unwelcome," said the rabbit. "Now do as I say or beat it."

"But happiness follows wherever I go!" the unicorn protested. "I can make a rainbow just by flicking my tail."

The rabbit reached for his stick.

"If you won't let me *through* the gate, I'll just jump over it," said the unicorn. And because he was taller than the rabbit and much more powerful, he did just that. "Sorry," he said as he headed into the forest, "but you didn't leave me any choice."

"We'll see about that," muttered the rabbit, and he spat onto the blood-soaked ground.

The unicorn spent the late afternoon making rainbows for all the woodland creatures. Then he caused the wildflowers to bloom and conjured up some berries for a hungry box turtle. As the sun set over the treetops, he settled upon a bed of fragrant moss and fell into a deep sleep.

The following morning, the songbirds woke him. The unicorn yawned and was just about to stand when he noticed the pile of golden shavings scattered across the moss. Then he felt his forehead and galloped to the gate piled high with rotting carcasses. "Who chewed off my horn?" he wailed.

The rabbit answered calmly that rules were rules. "If I let you trot around with a weapon on your head, I'd have to let everyone do it."

"But it had magic powers!"

"I said, scram," said the rabbit.

The unicorn, just a common everyday horse now, slunk off toward a field of tall grasses. The rabbit watched him go and then turned back to his sign. "Magic powers indeed," he muttered. "I didn't taste anything special." Again he spat, only this time, a diamond came out and landed on the ground beside him. That's what he was staring at when the wolves arrived.

The Judicious
Brown Chicken

It was hot that afternoon, so after the chicken and her sister had walked the yard a few times, they wandered into the henhouse for a little shade. Had it been crowded they probably wouldn't have said much, but there was no one around, and so the two spoke intimately, the way they had when they were young. "I don't know if it's normal or what," the sister said. "But sometimes . . . and this is just between the two of us, okay?"

The chicken nodded.

"Sometimes, when I'm with the rooster, I wonder what it would be like if he, you know, wasn't a rooster."

"You mean, like, if he was a duck or a goose?" The thought was ridiculous, and the chicken had to bite the inside of her beak to keep a straight face. "Or how about a turkey?" At this she lost her composure and whooped until her eyes teared. "I'm sorry," she said. "I'm sorry. Go on."

"Never mind," her sister said. "It wasn't important."

"Oh, don't be like that," the chicken scolded. "Come on, now. So if he's not a rooster, what is he?"

The sister took a deep breath and let it out slowly. "Well, like, maybe if he was, for instance, more like me?"

"Brown?" the chicken said, and in the silence that followed she grasped what her sister had been aiming at. "You don't mean . . ."

"It's just a thought," her sister said.

"Just a thought?"

"Something that's passed through my mind a couple of times."

"A couple of times?" This was what the chicken did when presented with shocking or unpleasant news. If informed, for example, of an outbreak of lice, she'd look at the speaker, saying, "An outbreak of lice?" as if the transformation from statement to question might somehow confuse the situation into reversing itself.

"I shouldn't have said anything," her sister said.

"Shouldn't have said anything?"

As they were talking, the farmer's wife walked in. She was a plump woman but quick, and before the sisters had time to run, she grabbed them by the feet and hung them upside down, one in each hand. The chicken had never seen the world from this angle and wasn't sure she liked it: an open doorway three feet off the ground. Trees hanging senselessly from a brilliant green sky. Her vision grew hazy, and just as she thought she might pass out, the farmer's wife released her grip and the chicken fell on her head into the straw. Her sister, meanwhile, with one clean jerk, had her neck wrung.

"At least it happened quickly," the gray pullet said, and the chicken agreed that it could have been worse.

"You're just lucky the woman chose your sister instead of you," the pullet continued, and though the chicken concurred, she knew that luck had nothing to do with it. Her sister had been killed because she deserved it — there was no other explanation. Decent creatures lived until they couldn't stand it anymore, and then they were ushered to a kind of paradise where they were adorned with jewels and tended to by servants hoisting platters full of grain.

Devious and perverse creatures, on the other hand, suffered untimely deaths and were sent to a reverse paradise where *they* were the servants, and instead of jewels they were adorned with flaming-hot coals. Her sister was there now, and all because she had entertained unnatural thoughts, which were as bad as unnatural actions in certain circumstances. "I'm sorry it had to happen," the chicken told the pullet, "but at least I learned something from it."

At dawn the following morning, the rooster made his rounds. He was a disagreeable character, someone to be endured rather than looked forward to, but to not accept him or to do so with less than a full heart was, the chicken now understood, a first-class ticket to hell. He approached her nest and had just taken his position when she turned to address him. "I want you to know," she whispered, "that I really love you."

"Tough titty," he said.

"No," she went on, "I mean it. Some of the

others, they might put up with you or whatnot, but I honestly treasure our time together, and I wouldn't trade you for anyone."

He told her that unless she was willing to talk dirty she should just keep her trap shut, and when she continued he jerked his head forward and pecked out her left eye.

"It was an accident," she told the others. "He gets excited and, well, you know, these things happen." Inwardly, though, she was devastated. Had the rooster chipped her beak, all right, no hard feelings, but her eyes were her best feature, and now she had only one of them. The other was just a dank hole, the rim crusted with blood and mucus.

"Cyclops," her friends started calling her. As in, "Hey, Cyclops, you might want to keep an eye out for that rooster." The only one who didn't tease her was an underweight guinea hen whom the chicken had seen around but never really spoken to. "I don't think it looks that bad, actually," she said. "I mean, it's part of what makes you *you*, right?"

The chicken had never thought about it this way and supposed the hen had a point. Though a missing eye was certainly nothing to be proud of, neither was it a reason to feel particularly ashamed.

"We've all got our little quirks," the guinea hen offered. "Some are visible, and others are on the inside, where no one can see them. Me, for instance, I'm super compassionate, was born that way, I suppose. If I see someone suffering, it just bothers the heck out of me, no matter who it is. This worm, for example, got bitten by a centipede, and I sat up half the night, comforting him until he died."

"But he was just a worm," the chicken said. "Why didn't you eat him?"

"Oh, I'm a vegetarian," the guinea hen explained. "Grain is good enough for me, but even then I never have more than a few kernels a day. What with all the starving songbirds struggling to feed their families, it hardly seems fair to take more than we need."

"But songbirds are trash," the chicken said, and the guinea hen laughed, saying, "Well, then, I guess we could all use a little more trash in our lives." She turned to admire a lark who perched singing on the low branch of a tree, and the chicken was struck by how thin she was and how her weight corresponded to a kind of inner peace. "Hello, little lark," the guinea hen said. "Are you having a nice day?"

"What's it to you, what's it to you, what's it to you?" the lark sang, and as the guinea hen offered her calm, beatific smile, a hawk swooped in and seized her in his mighty claws. The motion was fluid and almost beautiful. No beating of wings, just an effortless glide back into the sky and toward the distant treetops.

The lark roared with laughter, but the chicken used the incident as an opportunity to reflect and learn something. The hawk could just as easily have abducted her, but it did not. The question was, why? A less spiritual being might have taken a practical approach: the guinea hen was smaller and easier to carry. But that wasn't the answer, and the chicken knew it. The hen had been killed because she empathized too much and was strange to boot. "Everybody's different"; "Larks are worthy too." She should have spent more time eating and less time running her mouth, that was the lesson here, and the chicken intended to follow it. From now on she would consume twice as much and be twice as ashamed of her missing eye. On top of that she would love the rooster with all her heart and go out of her way to criticize songbirds, who were all a bunch of thieving hillbillies.

. . . .

A month after the guinea hen's death, the chicken was so heavy her thighs chafed. Her ankles hurt pretty much all the time, and her neck had been completely denuded by the rooster, who'd had it with what he called "That pissedy-assed love-talk shit." Something had moved into the hole formerly occupied by her left eye, but she refused to dwell on it. What few thoughts she allowed herself to entertain were reserved for the big things: death, mainly, and what might be learned in its aftermath. A fox stole into the henhouse one night and carried off the gray pullet, who screamed that she was too beautiful to die even as he was tearing a hole in her throat. *Vanity,* the chicken thought, and she swore off grooming herself or examining her reflection in the ditch. When a good-natured and sociable goose was struck by lightning, the chicken stopped talking altogether, much to the delight of the rooster.

"Gloomy," they started calling her, and she spent more and more time alone. She was by herself in the henhouse one morning when she saw a snake glide toward a nest and swallow an egg, the entire thing, whole. It hadn't been hers, but still she had to wonder what the unhatched chick had done to warrant such extreme punishment. It hadn't existed yet, so harboring unnatural thoughts was out, as was being excessively vain. Having lived alone inside its shell, it could hardly be accused of being too social or of eating any less than its fair share. The egg's crime, as far as she could see, was that it had been brown and roundish. *Just like me,* the chicken thought, and in that moment the farmer's wife came up from behind and grabbed her by the throat.

The Parrot and the Potbellied Pig

When asked why she'd chosen to become a journalist, the parrot was known to cock her head a half inch to the right and pause for a moment before repeating the question. "Why did I choose to become a journalist? Well, the easy answer is fairly obvious. Perfect recall is something I was born with, but I guess what really drives me is the money. That, and the free booze." It killed her to follow this with "I was just joking about the money."

The paper she worked at was called *The Eagle*, and she wrote for the Tempo section, which was later renamed Lifestyles and was now titled simply Living. Most of her stories were little more than puff pieces:

interview the wealthy tortoise who'd shelled out money for the new speedway; cover the benefit gala for feline leukemia research, for hip dysplasia, for ringworm or heartworm or the Hookworm Anti-Defamation League. She wanted an opportunity to show her chops, and finally got her break when a potbellied pig took over as director of the local art museum. *The Eagle* wanted something simple — three hundred words, tops — but the parrot thought differently and scheduled a long lunch.

Her guest arrived on time, and, after ordering, they got down to business. "So," the parrot began, "it's a long way from Ho Chi Minh City to the much-coveted director's chair of a noted museum. I'd like you to reminisce about the journey a little."

"I'm sorry," the pig said, "but I've never been to Ho Chi Minh City."

"But you are from that region, are you not?"

"No," the pig told her. "Not at all."

The parrot ran her fat black tongue over the ragged edge of her upper beak. "I don't mean to contradict you," she said, "but I've done a little leg-work, and it seems that you're officially registered with your health-care provider as a *Vietnamese* potbellied pig. So let's turn our thoughts eastward, shall we, and talk about your past."

"Technically, yes, I am a Vietnamese potbellied pig," the museum director said. "But that's just a silly formality. The fact is that I was born in this country, as were my parents, and their parents before them."

"I see," the parrot said, and she scratched the word "self-hating" in her notepad. "So how will your ethnicity reflect itself in regard to our museum? Can we expect to see more Oriental art? A pricey new Ming Wing perhaps? Some big 'Treasures of the Emperor' extravaganza?"

"Nothing's planned," the pig said.

"But you wouldn't rule it out?"

"Well, no, not completely, but —"

"That's all I wanted to know," the parrot said, and at that moment their lunch arrived.

It was she who had made the reservation, and in a flash of inspiration, she'd decided they'd go to Old Saigon. The fact that it was her idea would not be mentioned in the article. Nor would she add that the pig had never in his life used a pair of chopsticks and that he gripped them, one in each hoof, as if they were screwdrivers. During the meal — a few blades of lemongrass for him, a Mekong platter for her — they talked about this and that, but she wasn't really engaged, busy as she was dreaming up a headline. "Museum Takes on Asian Slant" was good, but she'd have to fight hard to get it past her editor, who despised what she called "wordplay."

When their lunch was over, the pig trotted back to the museum, and the parrot headed down to the VFW Hall, where she hoped to round out her article. There she spoke to a red-shouldered hawk who hadn't actually fought in Vietnam but who might have, had the war lasted just a few weeks longer. "I could have practically been killed over there, and now one of *them* is coming to *my* museum, trying to tell *me* what art I should look at?"

"I hear you," the parrot said.

The article was due the following morning, and she stayed up all night to finish it. Her editor scowled at the bulk of pages but softened after the first read-through, saying, "Good work, you" and "Maybe we should send this over to the city desk."

The eventual headline was no masterpiece — "Potbellied Museum Director Stirs Controversy"

— but the parrot was so relieved to move out of the Living section that the paper could have called it "Shit on a Stick" and she wouldn't have cared.

As for the pig, he wasn't nearly as upset as she'd thought he would be. Rather than threatening a lawsuit or demanding a retraction, he phoned to say that he was disappointed. "Deeply disappointed" were his exact words. The parrot reached for her pen, hoping for quotes that might lead to a second article. "Is that all you have to say?" she asked, and in response he sighed and gently hung up the phone.

"Hello?" the parrot said. "Hello? Hello?"

The pig would not have admitted it, but what really bothered him was the "potbellied" business. He had been plump all through his youth, and the years of name-calling had not just shaped his adult life but deformed it, like some cell made crazy by radiation. He couldn't remember the last time he had eaten without thinking — popped a passing canapé into his mouth, finished an entire potato chip or dry roasted peanut without calculating the damage. While others prepared for bed, he ran a treadmill. They tucked into their ample breakfasts, and he hung upside down from a bar in his living room, doubling at the waist until he saw stars. Then came the traditional sit-ups and half a slice of dry Ryvita before examining his silhouette in the hallway mirror and getting ready for work. His waist size was twenty-eight. His body-fat index was 2 percent. *He did not have a potbelly. He would never again have a potbelly.* Now here was this article, essentially comparing him to the Buddha.

After hanging up on the reporter, the pig began a three-day fast. Lunchtime came, and as his colleagues shuffled to the museum cafeteria, he sat at his desk and looked out the window at that stupid hawk, marching back and forth with his picket sign. The veteran had hoped that others might join him, but none of his fellows seemed to care. "The war is over, and it's time to move on," they'd been quoted as saying. "Who cares if some" — and there was that word again — "Who cares if some *potbellied* Charlie wants to hang pictures on a wall?"

"Damn that parrot from *The Eagle*!" The pig's anger felt vaguely nourishing, but he knew it was misplaced. The reporter hadn't assigned the ani-

mals their names; that was someone else's doing, someone who sat back and ordained — *largemouth bass, humpback whale, lesser wart-nosed horse-shoe bat* — not caring whose life was ruined.

By the time he next ran into the parrot, the pig had lost close to ten pounds. They met at a museum benefit, a costume ball that he hosted and that she hovered on the edges of, guzzling rum punch and gathering quotes she'd heard a thousand times before ("Wonderful party, and of course it's for such a good cause"). The parrot was, she liked to joke, "back with the Living, by which I mean section, not the sensation of being alive."

She'd assumed that the pig would be in disguise and was surprised to see him in the same dark suit he'd worn at the restaurant. He was standing at the bar, nursing a glass of water, and she came from behind and tapped him on the shoulder. "Let me guess," she said. "You're Henry Bacon, right?"

"Who's he?" the pig asked.

The parrot rolled her eyes. "American architect? Designed a little something called the Lincoln Memorial?"

"Oh," the pig said, "*that* Henry Bacon." He was going to admit that he was no one, or at least no one special, when the parrot stepped back and examined him again over the rim of her punch glass. "I've got it," she said. "You're Luther Hamm. Took the silver medal for the four-hundred-meter freestyle, Helsinki, nineteen fifty-two. Little wisp of a thing but, boy, did he have shoulders."

"Right," the pig said. "So who are you supposed to be?"

The parrot shrugged and held up her glass for a refill. "I thought I'd go all out and come as a two-bit journalist." For verification she presented an ink-stained claw, the nails of which were bitten to the quick. "So, hey," she added, "I'm sorry about the article. I haven't been that irresponsible since I worked in pirate radio. Broadcast journalism was never my thing, but you know how it is sometimes. You get pegged."

"That's all right," the pig told her.

"All right for you," the parrot said. "*I'm* the one with a goddamned hawk calling me every ten minutes. Now he wants to go after Middle Easterners. Heard of a Persian cat who runs a parking garage down by the Civic Center and is after me to write an 'exposé.'"

The pig laughed for the first time in months, and

then looked down to see the parrot's wing resting on his stomach. "Is it my imagination, or have you lost some weight?"

"No," he told her. "I mean, yes, I did. It's not your imagination."

He thought of how kind it was for her to mention it, and then he noticed how oddly satisfying it felt to be patted down by a wing.

Meanwhile, the parrot was still talking. "Don't get me wrong," she said. "I *have* seen a cockatoo in my time, but I'm not dating anyone now, if that's what you're wondering." She grabbed a passing appetizer, dumped the caviar back onto the tray, and ate only the cracker. "A cliché, I know, but fish eggs make me bloat."

"It's the salt," the pig told her. He'd hoped to say something more interesting, but just then the band started up.

A wolf in sheep's clothing called out for a fox-trot, and, as if a switch had been thrown, the party came to life. Here was the hare in cat's pajamas dancing with a chameleon, whose costume changed with every turn. The ugly duckling cut in on a swan. A trio of mice lowered their sunglasses, and as they scoured the floor for partners, the parrot turned to the pig and held out her claw. He accepted it awkwardly in his hoof, and so began what the reporter would later refer to as her days of swine and neuroses.

Hello Kitty

It was the stupidest thing the cat had ever heard of, an AA program in prison. Like you could find anything decent in here anyway. But if it would get his sentence reduced, well, all right, he'd sign up. Dance the twelve-step, do whatever it took to cut out early.

Once he was free he'd break into the nearest liquor store and start making up for lost time, but between now and then he'd sit with the sad sacks and get by with a little aftershave. The only thing he wouldn't do was speak at one of the meetings.

As a rule they were strictly dullsville. Yammer,

yammer, yammer, but every now and then someone would tell a decent story. This mink, for example, who'd swapped his own pelt for a bottle of Kahlúa. The cat didn't know you could survive without a pelt, but apparently it was possible. Not pretty, that was for damn sure, but it could be done, and this mink was living proof. It helped that he had a sense of humor about it and told his story with a little pizzazz, complete with sound effects and different voices. When he came to the bit about his wife mistaking him for a beef tongue, the cat laughed so hard he fell out of his chair.

"Thank you," the mink said at the end of his little speech. "You've been a terrific audience. Now don't forget to tip your waitress."

After the meeting, the alcoholics congregated for treats washed down with burnt coffee. The cat was just going back for a second cup when he overheard a mouse talking in a low voice to the bullfrog, who served as the prison chaplain. "He might be amusing, but I don't give that mink a snowball's chance in hell. In here, all right, but out in the real world, he's a ticking time bomb."

The cat didn't know what this mouse was in for, but he was willing to bet it was something boring:

fiddling with his taxes or mail fraud. He wouldn't know a good time if it slapped him between the ears, but here he was, ragging on the hairless mink: "Refuses to take his recovery seriously," "A classic example of a dry drunk."

Give the guy a break, the cat thought. *The poor bastard is permanently naked. His wife left him, his chop shop was confiscated, so who the hell cares if he starts drinking again? It beats wasting time with the likes of you.*

The cat didn't say any of these things, but he thought them, and it must have shown on his face.

"Do you have a problem?" the mouse asked.

And the cat said, "Yeah, as a matter of fact I do."

Sensing trouble, the chaplain moved between them and held out his webbed hands. "All right, gentlemen," he said, "let's just take this down a notch."

"I've got a problem with certain rodents," the cat continued. "The kind who think that unless you're as pompous as they are, you're going to wind up on the trash heap."

"Is that so?" the mouse said. "Well, I got a problem with cats who try to take someone else's inventory before they've taken their own."

He was a spunky little thing, you had to give him that. Here he was, no taller than a shot glass, yet he was more than willing to mix it up, and with a cat, no less. "Don't think I'm going to forget this," he said as the chaplain pulled him back.

And the cat said, "Oh, I'm so scared."

When dinnertime came, the cat joined the mink for burgers and fries in the prison cafeteria. The mouse was on the opposite side of the room, sitting between a rabbit and a box turtle at the vegetarian table, and every few seconds he'd look up from his plate and glare in the cat's direction.

"I don't know what's going on between you two," the mink said, "but you'd better find some friendly way to straighten it out. I'm telling you, brother, you do *not* want that mouse as an enemy."

"What's he going to do," the cat said, "steal the cheese off my hamburger patty?"

"I don't know what he's *going* to do, but I know what he *did* do," the mink said, and he leaned his raw, seeping head across the table. "They say it was arson. Chewed through some wires and set a police building on fire. Four German shepherds killed on the spot, and two more so burnt their own mothers wouldn't recognize them. Now, I don't know what *you'd* call it, but in my book, brother, that's cold."

The cat dragged a fry through a puddle of ketchup. "Dogs, you say?"

The mink nodded. "One of the burnt ones was two weeks from retirement. Had him a party lined up and everything."

"You're breaking my heart," the cat said.

The next AA meeting started like the rest of them. Not a decent story to be had. Someone said he was dying for a drink, and then someone else said the same thing. When that got repetitive, a member told the group *why* he wanted a drink. "Anyone else like to share?" the chaplain asked. "Any new voices we haven't heard from?"

The cat closed his eyes. He usually drifted off to sleep and came to during the serenity prayer, but today he stayed awake, waiting for the mouse to pipe up and say something stupid like "Easy does it" or "Fake it till you make it" — aphorisms he couldn't go two minutes without repeating. "Boys," he'd say, "when things get tough, I just have to remind myself to let go and let God."

Then everyone would act as if they hadn't heard

this five thousand times already. As if it weren't printed on flea collars, for Christ's sake.

Today, though, the mouse skipped the slogans and talked about a recent encounter that had tested his resolve. "I won't name names, but this was between myself and the sort of individual I call a nosey parker, the kind who likes to creep around and listen to conversations that are none of his business. That's how he gets his kicks, see."

The cat said, "Why, I oughtta —," and the chaplain pointed to a sign reading, NO CROSS TALK. Of all the rules, this was the lousiest, as it meant you couldn't directly respond, even when someone was obviously trashing you.

"Now, I didn't know this individual from Adam," the mouse continued. "I'd seen him around, sure, but aside from his plug-ugliness, there was no reason to take much notice. He was clearly no smarter than this chair I'm sitting on, but that didn't keep him from running his mouth — in fact, it was just the opposite. Pushed every button I have, he did, and just as I was about to rearrange his face, I remembered my fourth step and let it slide."

There was a general murmur of congratulations, and the mouse acknowledged it. "I can't say I'll be so forgiving the next time, but I guess I'll cross that bridge when I come to it."

Then a goat raised his hand and recalled getting drunk at his nephew's bar mitzvah. A guinea pig said some crap about insecurity, and a leech wondered if the Big Book came in an audio version. He'd just finished talking when the cat stuck his paw into the air, saying, "Hey, everybody, I got a little story to tell."

"That's not the way we do things here," the chaplain said. "Before you speak, you have to introduce yourself."

"Okay," the cat said. "I'm a cat, and I got a little story to tell."

"You know what I'm talking about," the chaplain said. "Come on, now, it's not going to kill you."

The cat stared across the table at the mouse and saw the same expression he'd observed the night before in the cafeteria: smirky, defiant — the look of someone convinced that he had already won.

"All right," the cat said. "I'm a cat and . . . aw, to hell with all of you."

The mouse put his little hand over his heart as if to say, "You're killing me," and the cat pounded his paw on the tabletop. "I'm a cat, all right. I'm a cat and I'm a . . . I'm a goddamn alcoholic. You happy now?"

Then everyone said, "Hello, Cat," and waited, their eyes politely downcast, as their fellow drunk, an official one now, struggled to regain his composure.

". . . So that's how I met my first sponsor," the cat would later say — this at meetings in damp church basements and low-slung community centers, years after he was released from prison. "That little SOB saved my life, can you beat that? A murderer, an arsonist, and not a day goes by when I don't think about him."

It maybe wasn't the best story in the world, but, as the mouse had told him on more than one occasion, it wasn't the worst either.

The Grieving Owl

I was flying past a house the other evening, and because the lights were off and there were no curtains on the ground-floor windows, I stopped to take a peek inside — which I do sometimes, just to see how people decorate. This particular place was made of stone, not old, just made to *look* old, with a reproduction carriage lamp in the front yard and one of those roofs that appear to be slate but are actually made of recycled rubber. From the outside it screamed *Wagon Wheel Coffee Table*, but it turns out they had some pretty nice furniture, at least in the living room. A lot of painted pine — English, from the looks of it.

From there I peered into what's called the den. That's a room where people go to be themselves — or at least some idea of themselves. You see a lot of boats in dens, but in this one the theme was owls. Not real ones — I don't think I could have handled that — but representations, both flat and three-dimensional: Screech-owl andirons, a candle in the likeness of a white barn owl. Above the mantel was a rather clumsy painting of a snowy owl hovering above a cross-eyed ferret, and on the desk, a small figurine of a great horned owl. Take away its glasses and the mortarboard cocked just so on his head, and it was me. Or perhaps I'm being too egotistical. It wasn't *just* me. It was my mother, my brother, my sister and cousins. Everyone, basically, who I'm trying to get away from.

It's not just that they're stupid, my family — that, I could forgive. It's that they're actively *against* knowledge — opposed to it the way that cats, say, are opposed to swimming, or turtles have taken a stand against mountain climbing. All they talk about is food, food, food, which *can* be interesting but usually isn't.

There are, of course, exceptions. I once had a

fascinating conversation with a seagull who was quite the authority on the subject of the French-fried potato. I always thought they were all the same, but not so apparently. To hear her tell it, the taste varies according to what sort of oil is used.

I said, "What *sort?*" Who knew there was more than one kind of oil! Then there's the question of texture, with crisp on one end and soggy on the other. The type of potato makes a difference as well, as does its age and exposure to the elements.

Following our talk, I went on a restaurant jag. Every night I'd pick a new one and look through the windows into their kitchens. What I saw, aside from the ovens and so forth, were a lot of mice. This kept me going back to restaurants and led to an encounter, the night before last, in the parking lot of a steak house. There I came upon a rat making his way toward the back door. "Not so fast, friend," I said.

One of the things an owl learns early is *never engage with the prey.* It's good advice if you want to eat and continue to feel good about yourself. Catch the thing and kill it immediately, and you can believe that it *wanted* to die, that the life it led — this

mean little exercise in scratching the earth or col-
lecting seeds from pods — was not a *real* life but
just some pale imitation of it. The drawback is that
you learn nothing new.

So this rat, it was as if he were following a script.
"I just swallowed some poison," he claimed. "Eat
me, and you're destined to die as well."

It's embarrassing to hear such lies, to think *they*
think you're dumb enough to believe them.

"Oh please," I said.

The rat moved to plan B. "I have children,
babies, and they're counting on me to feed them."

I said to the guy, "Listen. There's not a male rat
in the history of the world who's given his child so
much as a cigarette butt, and don't try to tell me
otherwise. In fact," I went on, "from what I hear,
any baby of yours has a better chance of being eaten
by you than fed by you."

"True enough," the rat admitted. His body relaxed beneath my talons, and I felt his hope leak
onto the asphalt, as surely as if it were blood or
urine.

"I'll make you a deal," I said. "Teach me something new, and I'll let you go."

"This is a joke, right?" the rat said.

"No," I told him. "I mean it. You tell me something, and if I find it interesting, I'll release you." This was how I'd learned about dens and English furniture, about roof tiles and vegetable oil and reproduction carriage lamps.

"All right," said the rat, and he paused, thinking. "Did you know that all this restaurant's shrimp are frozen?"

"No, I didn't, but that's not really good enough," I told him. "Nothing that goes on in a steak house would surprise me, especially if it's a chain. You need to think farther afield."

"Okay," he said, and he told me about the time he tried to have sex with his mother.

"How is that supposed to help me be a more well-rounded individual?" I asked. "Don't you know anything *important?*"

Then he told me that there's a certain kind of leech that can only live in the anus of a hippopotamus.

"Get out of town," I said.

"No, honest," he swore. "I had an uncle who lived at the zoo, and he heard it firsthand from the hippo herself."

It was one of those things so far-fetched it simply had to be true. "All right," I said, and I lifted my foot off his back. "You are free to go."

The rat took off across the parking lot, and just as he reached the restaurant's back door, my pill of a brother swooped down and carried him away. It seemed he had been following me, just as, a week earlier, I'd been trailed by my older sister, who ate the kitten I had just interrogated, the one who taught me the difference between regular yarn and angora, which is reportedly just that much softer.

"Who's the smart one now?" my brother hooted as he flew off over the steak house. I might have given chase, but the rat was already dead — done in, surely, by my brother's talons the second he snatched him up. This has become a game for certain members of my family. Rather than hunt their own prey, they trail behind me and eat whoever it was I'd just been talking to. "It saves me time," my sister explained after last week's kitten episode.

With the few hours she saved, I imagine she sat on a branch and blinked, not a thought in her empty head.

After my brother took off with the rat, I flew to a telephone pole on the far end of the parking lot. A leech that lives in the anus of a hippopotamus. Talk about a closed society! What must it be like to live like that, your family within spitting distance your entire life?

My next stop was the city zoo. I've heard there are some that house the animals in actual landscapes, fields and jungles and the like. Ours, I discovered, is more old-fashioned, geared toward the viewer rather than the viewed. The panther's cage is about the size of an eighteen-wheel truck. Our lions have it a little better, but then there are two of them. I don't know how much territory a hippo might require in the wild, but here at the zoo her pen is on the small side, not even as big as a volleyball court. There's a pool for her to submerge herself in, and the ground around it is paved in cement. A sign in front of her display reads, LOIS, but that, she explained, was just her slave name. "I don't go by anything, not now, not ever," she told me. "It's just not the hippo way."

What struck me right off was her warmth and accessibility. You expect this with miniature goats, but hippos, I'd heard, were notoriously grumpy.

"Oh, I have my moments," this one said, and she started talking about her teeth. They looked like pegs hammered at random into her gums, and it seemed that one of them had been giving her trouble — which is not to make her sound like a complainer, far from it. "It's not all bad, living in the zoo," she told me. "True, I don't have much space, but at least it's all mine. For a while last year they brought in a male, trucked him over from some wildlife center in the hopes we'd get it on and have a baby, but the pregnancy didn't happen, which was fine by me. It's not that I don't want kids, I just don't want them *now*, if you get what I'm saying?"

"Sure."

"So anyway, how about you?"

I told her that great horned owls hook up for life, a rarity in the bird world. My mate passed away before our first clutch of eggs could hatch, but I learned a while ago that it's best to keep this to myself. "A mood killer" is what the seagull diplomatically called it. And it's true. Someone tells you his mate died, was struck by an ambulance, no less, and of course it casts a pall. That's why I didn't mention it to the hippo — I wanted to spare her the awkwardness.

What else did we talk about the night we first met? I remember she asked what the land surrounding the zoo was like. She thought it was all trees and winding paths; little wooden huts selling balloons and cotton candy — that everything looked like what she saw from the bars of her pen. The hippo didn't know about muffler shops and office-supply superstores, about restaurants and motels and apartment complexes with pools lit by underwater lamps.

What does the world look like? "Well," I told her, "that's going to take a while."

"That's what I was hoping," she said.

On my way home that night, I picked up a rabbit. It was on the small side, and no sooner had I started eating than my mother appeared. "I'll wait until you're finished," she said in that particular way that means *What kind of son can't offer his mother so much as an appendage?* Sighing, I ripped off an ear and passed it over.

"You shouldn't have," she said. Then, her mouth full, she brought up one of my cousins who's single and will soon reach breeding age. Despite my opposition, my mother is determined to find me a new mate. "There's been talk," she keeps saying. But what talk? From who?

My former mate had been dead for all of three days when my mother set me up with the daughter of one of her neighbors. We met at dawn, in a big oak overlooking a pasture. Below us on the grass, a white calf took her mother's teat in her mouth, and my date shouted, "Faggot!"

"I think the word you're looking for is 'lesbian,' " I said. "Though even that wouldn't make sense. What they're doing isn't sexual — it's called nursing. It's the way mammals feed their young."

She said, "Yeah, *faggot* mammals."

When I told this to my mother, she looked at the bloody rabbit I was holding and said only "What about the other ear?" Then she swore that this new female, my cousin, was different. "I told her you'd meet her tomorrow night, on top of the cross in front of God Saint Christ Jesus Lord." This is her name for the Catholic church, which is actually — I've told her a thousand times — called Saint Timothy's. Not that it mattered in this case. At eleven o'clock the following evening, I was back at the zoo, talking to the hippo.

We started that night by discussing the pigeons

and sparrows who come in the day and defecate on the concrete surrounding her pool. "Disgusting," she said. "If there's one thing I can't stand, it's a goddamn bir —" She caught herself. "Bir . . . thday."

"You can't stand *birthdays?*"

"It's the fuss," she said. "I mean, who needs it?"

"Listen," I told her, "don't worry about hurting my feelings. With one or two exceptions, I'm not much for birds either." Then I told her about the seagull I'd met, the one who taught me about French-fried potatoes. "A while after her I ran into a rat, who said, and correct me if I'm wrong, that there's a certain type of leech that can only live in your, uh, rectum."

"I don't know if that's the *only* place they can live, but I know I've had them back there for a good nine months," the hippo said. "Little sons of bitches is what they are. I think I picked them up from that two-bit Romeo they sent from the wildlife center."

"Do they hurt?"

"Not so much," she said. "It's more the principle, if you know what I mean. The idea that they can just live inside me, rent free, like they own the place." She looked behind her as far as she could. "Then too, they're loud."

"You can hear them talking?"

"Not the exact words," she said. "It's more of a constant, low-level murmur. It's even more noticeable when I'm under water."

"What do you *think* they talk about?" I asked.

"Oh, regular asshole things," the hippo said. "I don't mean things about *my* asshole but the sorts of things that low-life assholes are interested in — incest, maybe, or cards."

"Cards?"

She nodded her massive head. "The men who clean my pen like to play them on their breaks. Sometimes they sit on the bench beside the snack hut, and I watch."

Off in the distance, the panther screamed. Then I heard a police siren. "If you wanted, I could maybe listen to what they're saying," I offered.

"I don't know that I want to give them that much importance," the hippo said.

"Fair enough," I told her, and I tried to tamp down my disappointment. *How can you not want to know what your parasites are talking about?* I wondered.

"What if what they're saying is cruel?" she continued. "It's bad enough having them in there, but if they're literally making fun of me behind my back, it would be too much to bear."

"It's equally possible they could be trying to thank you," I said. "I mean, just because they're leeches doesn't mean they're ungrateful."

"Isn't that sort of *exactly* what it means?" she asked.

I had just conceded her point when her curiosity got the better of her and she agreed to take me up on my offer. "If what they're saying is awful, though, I don't want to know the specifics."

There was a short concrete platform near the front of her pen, and at her suggestion I stood upon it while she backed up. This brought her bottom level with my head, which I then cocked and brought as close as I could to her anus. "Raise your tail," I said.

The hippo did, and I heard what sounded at first like a rabble, many voices talking over one another. Then I realized that they weren't talking.

"Let me get this straight," the hippo said when I explained what was going on. "Leeches are *singing* inside my asshole."

"To the best of my knowledge, yes," I told her.

"It's so much fun in there that they've *broken into song?*"

"It could just be the way they communicate," I offered. "Maybe this is what they do when they're sad or angry." It didn't sound much like a dirge, though. More like a German drinking number.

"I want them out and I want them out *now,*" the hippo said, her voice so forceful the platform trembled.

"Look," I told her, "there's obviously nothing we can do right this minute, so let's both sleep on it and see how things look tomorrow night."

On my way home that evening, I swooped low over a suburban driveway and caught what turned out to be a gerbil. Funny-looking thing — slight, with a brushlike tail and a scrap of red fabric around her midsection. I had planned to grab a quick bite and go home to bed, but something this potentially interesting — it would be a shame to just kill it.

"Hold on, friend," I said, and after her brief and pointless struggle, I learned that she was an escaped pet. An only child had kept her prisoner in her bedroom and was attempting to dress her in a doll-size bikini when the gerbil bit the girl on the hand and made a run for it. "For a few hours I hid beneath the refrigerator," she told me. "That seemed too obvious, though, so I moved into a copper pipe in back of the hot water heater, the old disconnected one they keep in their mudroom, the slobs."

It was so much new information: A mudroom! A bikini! A hot water heater! "How big was the pipe?" I asked.

The gerbil told me it was narrower than she was. "Not a problem for tunnel dwellers such as myself," she said. "Truth be told, I like a tight fit." She glared at the bikini top, then added, "Within reason."

Just as I realized the gerbil's potential value, I heard a beating of wings and turned to see my sister standing behind me. A moment later my brother landed. "What have we got here?" he asked.

"Looks like a mouse with a messed-up tail," said my sister. "Or a little squirrel, maybe, that was rained on."

"Actually, I'm a gerbil," the gerbil said. I wasn't expecting her to join the conversation, but hearing her voice — so full of pride and sass — made me feel right about sparing her. "If you've never come upon one of me before, it's because I'm not native to this area. I'm" — and she said the greatest thing — "invasive."

My brother moved a step closer to my sister and asked if that was another word for "dressed up."

"I'm pretty sure. Yeah," she answered.

The gerbil looked from one of them to the other. Then she turned to me. "Wow, these two are stupid," she said. "No dumber than hamsters, I'll grant them that, but you hear about owls and automatically think 'brainy.' "

"That's just a myth," I told her, and then, before my dumbfounded brother and sister, I lifted the gerbil in my right talon and took off. Figuring my family would probably come looking for us, I flew past my home and headed to a henhouse on an abandoned farm out near the reform school. There I helped the gerbil remove her bikini top and watched as she hunkered down, exhausted, in a pile of hay. It would have been easy for her to run away, but I hoped she would stay put. More than hoped actually. I meant to say something to this effect, but then I must have dropped off.

It wasn't much later that I awoke — the story of my life since my mate passed away. I get tired, wiped out, even, but can't seem to sleep more than a few hours at a stretch. It's such a weird time to be awake — noon. Spooky, really. There have been a few occasions when, tired of just standing there and hoping to fall back to sleep, I got up and flew around.

The dining options were definitely interesting — lapdogs, ducklings, I even saw an iguana sunning himself on top of a Styrofoam cooler. But there was also a lot of traffic and noise.

I never liked the world I saw during the day. Then I started hating the one I saw at night and wondered, *What's left?* What changed things, albeit slowly, was learning. It's like there's a hole where my life used to be, and I'm filling it with information — about potatoes. About hot water heaters. Anything will do. These leeches, though. For the first time in memory, I was unable to sleep not because I was anxious but because I was excited. To live in a damp crowded asshole and sing — if these guys don't know the secret to living, I don't know who does.

The gerbil awoke just after sunset and busied herself hunting crickets. After that I took her to a bird feeder, where she put away a few dozen sunflower seeds. Then she wiped her mouth and turned to me, saying, "Okay, Owl, what's the plan?"

A short while later we were at the zoo, where I introduced her to the hippopotamus. The two hit it off immediately, and within minutes the gerbil was all caught up vis-à-vis the anal parasites. "Fascinating!" she said. "And you're telling me they *sing?*"

"I want them out," repeated the hippo, and with no hesitation the gerbil offered to go in after them. "Why not?" she said. "I've been in tighter places — no offense — and if I can't convince them to leave, I can at least find out what their story is."

"You would do that for me?" the hippo asked.

The gerbil answered that she'd just spent eighteen months living in a cage. "When I finally escaped, I told myself that from here on out, I was going to make some changes: try new food, visit exotic places, live a little!"

I couldn't believe what a good sport she was. I'd have wanted time to mentally prepare, but not her. The only suggestion she made was that we lube her up a little. "Just to give me a bit more mobility."

"You think?" the hippo said. "But what about your fur?"

And the gerbil laughed, saying, "This old thing?"

There was a carousel near the entrance to the

zoo. The gears were coated in heavy grease, and after the gerbil had rubbed against them, I returned her to the pen, where we positioned ourselves on the concrete platform. The hippo backed up under my direction, and though it took quite a bit of maneuvering, we eventually got her rectum even with the gerbil. She was just about to crawl in when I felt myself being watched, and looked up to see four pairs of eyes, perfectly round and glinting from a tree beside the snack hut. My mother was there, my brother and sister, and joining them was, I'm willing to guess, the cousin I'd stood up last night. Then an elderly uncle arrived. Then an aunt.

I used to think that there were great horned owls and not-so-great horned owls. I'd put my former mate and myself in the first category, and from that lofty vantage point, we'd looked down upon my family. Now they were looking down on *me:* A son. A brother. A cousin, a nephew, a half-baked know-it-all standing beside a grease-blackened gerbil at the gaping back door of a hippopotamus. Even discounting the singing leeches, it really was stunning: this trio of newfound friends, so far-fetched we simply had to be true.

The Vomit-Eating Flies

The fly was at the bus station when he saw a man in a sailor suit clutch his stomach. Then he leaned forward in his plastic seat and vomited onto the scuffed linoleum floor. "Son of a bitch," the man muttered, and he wiped his mouth with the back of his hand. "I just paid six dollars for that!"

There was a bathroom next to the snack bar, and as the man rose unsteadily to his feet and stumbled in its direction, the people flanking him abandoned their seats, leaving a wide berth for what looked to be an excellent meal. The fly liked a hot lunch and was just tucking in when a second fly, this one a female, flew down from the ceiling and landed on a narrow peninsula beside him. "What have we got here?" she asked.

"Chinese," the male said.

The female sighed and picked halfheartedly at a snow pea. "Ten will get you twenty it's from the Shanghai Garden," she told him. "I had their pork lo mein once and was in the restroom for two days."

"Well, I don't mind it," the male said, and he moved from a beef chunk to a sliver of ginger. "If you don't like ethnic, there are some potato chips in here too. And a grilled cheese sandwich."

"What kind of cheese?" the female asked. "If it's American, you can have it."

"Suit yourself," the male said.

"By law, they shouldn't even be calling it cheese, that's how tasteless and full of chemicals it is." The female glanced into a slick of digestive juices and saw her face multiplied a hundredfold, scowling back at her. "Anyway, when it comes to regurgitated food, you really need to consider the source — the class of person or dog or whatever. Take the lieutenant governor and his family, for example, whom I happen to know quite intimately."

"Do you?" the male said. He had no idea what a lieutenant governor was, but out of politeness he made himself sound interested, the way he did when someone spoke about computers or yoga.

"Oh yes," said the female. "Why, I was practically raised at Old Stoney, which is what they call their summer home on the lake. The lieutenant governor's wife — Khaki, to her friends — is two months pregnant, though that's strictly on the Q.T., at least until the formal announcement is made. She suffers from the most terrible morning sickness, and her vomit is outstanding, better than normal spoiled food, in my opinion!"

"You don't say," said the fly.

"Her feces were good as well, at least what I could get of them," the female continued. "Like most people of good breeding, Khaki uses a toilet, but then some horrible journalist wrote that she'd had a cocaine problem in college, so she defecated into a shoe box. The plan was to mail it to him at the newspaper, and while she pieced together a note I swooped in for a quick taste."

"And?"

"Excellent," the female said. "The best feces I've ever had. Almost like dessert."

The fly pointed in the direction of the departure board. "If it's sweet you're after, there's a bit of jam smeared on that handrail over near the front door. I also saw a peach pit on the ground next to the trash can."

"I meant *inherently* sweet, spiritually sweet," the female said. "It's a quality the lieutenant governor's wife has in spades. As has Monica Van Landingham."

The fly looked at her blankly.

"The actress? Monica Van Landingham? Winner of two Spotlight Awards?"

"Sorry," confessed the fly.

"Well, she's a very important person," the female told him. "Extremely important. We met when she was an overnight guest at Old Stoney — not more than five days ago, it was. There was a fund-raising ball for the upcoming election. Miss Van Landingham's shoes were too tight, so of course she developed a blood blister and of course it popped on the brand-new ottoman the moment she returned to her room to put her poor swollen feet up. I tried to clean it off before she noticed, but she's quick, Miss Van Landingham. Observant too, so I got no more than five or six mouthfuls before she dabbed at it with soap and water. That did nothing to get the blood out, so in the end she blamed it on the lieutenant governor's dog, Chocolate Chip, which may *seem* dishonest but isn't, really, seeing as he may as well have done it. It's such a common breed, the Jack Russell." She picked at a bit of onion. "I can't believe you don't know who Monica Van Landingham is."

"I'm actually more of a barfly," the male told her. "Certain sports figures I could maybe recognize, but otherwise I don't have a clue." He wanted to add that he didn't care either. Life was short — with luck, you had maybe thirty days — so what did it matter whose crap you were eating? The same was true for vomit and blood blisters: just eat and shut up about it, for God's sake.

"Perhaps you've seen Miss Van Landingham on TV, then," the female said. "Not on a commercial — she'd never stoop so low — but on the news. You might think that's odd for an actress, but she has opinions — important ones. Just last week, to give you an example, she came out against breast cancer — told the world, 'Hey, I think it's a bad idea!'"

"Well, that's great," the fly said.

"Call me crazy, but I'm against it too," the female announced. "I'm against breast cancer and drunk driving and the one where kids in other countries get their feet blown off. And it's not just my association with Khaki and Miss Van Landingham — I'd be against these things anyway."

On the other side of the room, a door opened, and from it stepped a janitor with a mop in a rolling bucket. "Just my luck," muttered the fly, and he quickened his pace while monitoring the man's progress.

"Tonight there's a benefit for people who can't count," the female told him. "It's black tie, and everyone will be there. Everyone important anyway. I'm just waiting until it begins." She paused. "That's not an invitation, mind you. I just figured you were wondering what someone like me was doing at the bus station."

"That, I was," said the fly, and he watched over her head as the janitor lifted his mop. "Especially someone like you, with American cheese stuck to her chin."

"Oh my God," said the female. "How long has it been there?" She dipped her front legs into a puddle of grease, and just as she'd begun to wash her face, the mop came down, and the fly took off for the other side of the room, where a woman in a straw hat had placed an uncovered Tupperware dish upon her suitcase. He parked himself on the NO SMOKING sign above her head, and watched while the janitor ruined a perfectly good meal.

As for the female, he wasn't going to waste any time feeling guilty. *Constant vigilance* — that was a fly's motto, and woe be to anyone who let her attention waver, no matter how good-looking she was. He had to give the female that, at least. She had been pretty. If she'd known how to keep her trap shut, he might have upped her to beautiful, but wasn't that always the way with the ladies? For every good quality they possessed, there were two bad ones just waiting to be discovered.

The male waited another few seconds, and when the woman below shut her eyes for a nap, he moved a bit closer and saw that what she'd set atop her suitcase was pie. Blueberry, and almost an entire slice. A fellow could spend the rest of his life eating a thing like this. He might not finish it — might not even come close — but neither would he grow tired of it, the way he might of vomit or rot or even fresh feces. Such succulent bounty, and all of it for him! The fly was rubbing his hands together, just preparing to tuck in, when he heard a familiar voice and looked up to see the female. "Talk about a close call!" she said, and she shook a bead of mop water off her wing. "Now, where was I?"

As the fly bit glumly into his favorite filling, she positioned herself in a sunbeam and resumed her monologue from the vantage point of the upper crust.

About the Illustrator

Ian Falconer is the author and illustrator of the bestselling Olivia series: *Olivia,* a 2001 Caldecott Honor Book; *Olivia Saves the Circus; Olivia . . . and the Missing Toy; Olivia Forms a Band; Olivia Helps with Christmas;* and *Olivia Goes to Venice* (2010). His illustrations have also graced many covers of *The New Yorker.* In addition, he has designed sets and costumes for the New York City Ballet, the San Francisco Opera, and the Royal Opera House (Covent Garden), among others. He lives in New York City.

About the Author

David Sedaris is a regular contributor to *The New Yorker* and Public Radio International's *This American Life*. His books have been translated into twenty-six languages.

ALSO BY DAVID SEDARIS

Barrel Fever

"Shrewd, wickedly funny. . . . These hilarious, lively, and breathtakingly irrelevant stories . . . move way too fast to be summarized or described. They made me laugh out loud more often than anything I'd read in years."
— Francine Prose, *Washington Post Book World*

"Fortunately, not every page of *Barrel Fever* will leave you laughing so hard it's impossible to breathe — thank goodness for the droll but manageable Table of Contents — but still, this is one of those 'Open at your own risk' books. . . . *Barrel Fever* is wacky writing par excellence: original, acid, and wild." — Michael Dorris, *Los Angeles Times*

Back Bay Books • Available wherever paperbacks are sold

ALSO BY DAVID SEDARIS

Naked

"Brilliant.... A fresh comic voice.... There's wisdom in these stories."   — Paula Chin, *People*

"Not one of the seventeen autobiographical essays in this collection failed to crack me up; frequently I was helpless. . . . Even the bleakest of them contain stuff you shouldn't read with your mouth full."
— Craig Seligman,
New York Times Book Review

"Sedaris's prose is fierce and funny, full of feeling yet unsentimental. He brings people's flaws and foibles into a harsh and unforgiving light, often to delicious comic effect."   —Sam Hurwitt,
San Francisco Examiner

Back Bay Books • Available wherever paperbacks are sold

ALSO BY DAVID SEDARIS

Holidays on Ice

Twelve of David Sedaris's most profound holiday stories — collected in one slender volume perfect for use as a last-minute coaster or ice scraper.

"Not remotely politically correct or heartwarming."
— Liesl Schillinger, *New York Times*

"No one is funnier or more wistfully absurd than David Sedaris."   — *Newsday*